Swimming Made Easy

Also by Terry Laughlin:

Books:

The Swimmer's Bible

The Swiminar Workbook

The Guide to Fishlike Swimming

Total Immersion:
The Revolutionary Way to Swim Better, Faster, and Easier

The Total Immersion Pool Primer: Freestyle and Backstroke

Videos:

Freestyle and Backstroke: The Total Immersion Way

Butterfly and Breaststroke: The Total Immersion Way

Swimming Made Easy

The *Total Immersion* Way for *Any* Swimmer
to Achieve Fluency, Ease, and Speed
in *Any* Stroke

TM

Terry Laughlin

Swimware, Inc.
New Paltz, NY

ISBN 1-931009-01-5

For more information about Terry Laughlin's Total Immersion swim workshops, call 800-609-7946.

Text and concept: Terry Laughlin
Editing and photography: Barbara Tomchin
Design, graphics, and technical contributor: Glenn Mills

Published by Swimware, Inc., a division of Total Immersion, Inc.
171 Main Street
New Paltz, NY 12561

First edition published 2001
Printed in the United States of America

10 9 8 7 6 5 4 3 2 1

This book is dedicated to all of those Total Immersion swimmers who have welcomed our books and videos, and particularly those who have attended our clinics, camps, and workshops since 1989. They have taught me far more about swimming than I ever imagined possible, and their curiosity and eagerness to learn have been a constant source of inspiration, allowing me to spend countless fulfilling hours working on deck at what I consider to be the best swim-coaching job in the world. Thank you.

Contents

Foreword

Total Immersion: The Next Step

Total Immersion has been publishing guidebooks for swimmers since 1991. We started with a slim book, immodestly titled *The Swimmer's Bible*, followed in 1994 by the *Swiminar Workbook*, which in 1997 was updated as *The Guide to Fishlike Swimming*. In 1996, Simon and Schuster published *Total Immersion: The Revolutionary Way to Swim Better, Faster, and Easier.* The reaction by readers to each of these books has been the same: "Thanks for writing about swimming IN A WAY THAT MAKES SENSE!" It has been my constant goal to do just that. After reading far too many books and articles (and hearing countless coaching-clinic presentations) that portrayed swimming excellence as rocket science, I really hoped to provide a swimming-improvement method that anyone could understand and follow.

Feedback from countless "TI fans" has confirmed that we're on the right track. Enthusiasm for the TI approach – from all manner of swimmers, from novices to elites (and coaches and teachers, too) -- has been greater than I've ever witnessed in 30-plus years as swimmer, coach, and student of the sport. There is only one reason for this: OUR METHODS WORK. It doesn't matter if the swimmer is age 3 or 43 or 73 — or whether they've never swum before or have swum their way to the Olympics. What we teach — and the simple, clear way in which we teach it — can turn anyone into a swimmer or make them a better swimmer than they are now.

TI for Every Stroke

Our previous books have focused exclusively on freestyle – though many of their lessons could be applied to any swimming style. This book is our first comprehensive written guide for becoming "fishlike" in all four strokes. The learning process that produced it is precisely the same as the one that preceded our books about swimming a fishlike freestyle: We went to the pool and taught hundreds of swimmers of all types. Since 1997, we have taught summer camps for swimmers age 8 to 17 and have added four-stroke weekend workshops. In all cases, we've had to get across the essentials of fluent swimming – the techniques that *really* matter – in just a few days while also preparing our students to coach themselves, and we had to do so for four strokes, not just one. So the need to streamline and simplify (and eliminate steps that are not truly essential and productive) has been even greater for the other strokes than it has been for freestyle.

At the same time, dozens of coaches who have adopted TI methods in their own age-group, high school, college, and Masters programs have shared their insights and discoveries to help us refine what we developed in the workshops. And finally, from 1996 to 1999, I coached Division I collegiate swimmers at the US Military Academy – West Point. I worked primarily with the sprinters, coaching and teaching all four strokes, and found that the TI approach was equally effective with already accomplished college swimmers who needed to compete on the highest level.

One of the best rewards of teaching the other strokes is that our understanding of how to teach a fishlike freestyle has also improved, both generally and specifically. The exercise of teaching four strokes, rather than one, has shown us many additional ways to teach swimmers to be fluent. It has also brought an unexpected benefit: We have found that improved awareness of how to flow with and through the water can help *any* swimmer learn to swim *any* stroke better.

So, the good news is that if you've already learned to swim a better freestyle with our previous books and videos, this book – and the accompanying videos covering freestyle/backstroke and breaststroke/butterfly – will bring you a whole new series of methods and approaches that can make you a more complete swimmer *and* make your freestyle faster, easier, and more fluent.

Finally, our thanks for allowing us the opportunity to help you improve your swimming. Without the thousands of faithful TI followers coming to us for instruction and providing invaluable feedback, we certainly would not have been able to learn all we have about how to make swimming a more joyful and satisfying experience.

Acknowledgments

To my family -- Alice, Fiona, Cari, and Betsy -- for their patience, support, and love.

To my Total Immersion colleagues -- Glenn Mills, Barbara Tomchin, Tammy Martin, and Katie Elliot -- for helping to make this work fun and interesting, for providing ideas and inspiration, and for freeing me to do what I do best: teach swimming and write about it.

To my dozens of TI coaching colleagues (also including Glenn and Barbara) for contributing priceless ideas and insights and for sharing in the spirit of exploration of how coaching can be done.

To John Delves for acting, once again, as my "surrogate reader" and in helping the text in this book flow like the strokes we are teaching.

To the swimmers I coached at West Point from 1996 to 1999 for helping me to demonstrate that TI works just as well with fast and accomplished swimmers as it does with novices, and for helping refine its application to all four strokes.

To Brian Williams, head coach of the SUNY New Paltz swim team, for generously allowing us to use the SUNY facilities for our filming.

Introduction

Swimming Reinvented:
What Makes Total Immersion
Totally Different

What sets Total Immersion apart from all other swim-improvement methods? Just about everything. Our instruction is unlike any other you may have experienced, and it's different from the ground up. From the very beginning, we actually ask you to go against your most basic, inbred instincts to get the results you want. That's because whatever humankind's evolutionary origins (they say we're evolved from aquatic creatures), *Homo sapiens* today are designed to move around comfortably on land. We've lost our aquatic instincts and replaced them with the ones we need on land. But it is possible to relearn aquatic instincts with the right training. And when you do, you'll be astonished at what happens next.

In the process, you'll be joining the thousands of improvement-minded swimmers we've had the good fortune to teach over the past 10 years. Working closely with so many highly motivated students has led us to a series of rare and unexpected insights that have gradually strengthened the core principles of our instruction. The result? A thoroughly unconventional way of teaching swimming that is different not because we like being different, but because it works. Our unique approach lets people improve far more quickly and easily, and turns them into swimmers who are not only faster and more efficient, but also satisfying to watch. TI swimmers are instantly recognized — and envied — for their grace in the water, whether they are children or adults new to the sport, or elite-level athletes, or Navy SEALS, or SCUBA divers.

More than anything else, that's because **we teach "fishlike" swimming**, which focuses on learning to be comfortable, slippery, and fluent in the water. Others teach "human" swimming, which means you laboriously muscle your way through the water by pulling and kicking, and do it over and over again for endless laps that are supposed to condition you for — more pulling and kicking.

A few lucky people are born with an inner "water sense" that tips them off right away that muscling through the water is not the smart way to swim. But this kind of inner water sense is rare. In fact, experience with thousands of students has led us to formulate **"The Rule of Two Percent,"** which says that only about one person in fifty has the native ability to swim fluently without *unlearning* bad habits or instincts. The other 98 percent of us (counting only those who can swim well enough to do at least a few laps nonstop) follow our instincts and struggle along unnecessarily, working hard mainly to make our bad habits more permanent. To swim well, we first need to forget everything we "know" about swimming, because virtually *everything* you do by instinct in the water tends to be clumsy, inefficient, and exhausting. And the more you swim instinctively, the more you perfect your "struggling skills." It didn't take us long, as we initially developed our program of fishlike swimming, to realize we were teaching people to do things that they would never do on their own. We had to find ways to let students replace clumsy human-swimming instincts with graceful, fishlike habits.

Soon, we came to understand that we were teaching what you might call **"martial-arts swimming."** That's because moving through the water like a fish is a fine, subtle, and — in the beginning — elusive skill. It is a "movement art" that requires you to cultivate body awareness, balance, and flow. And just as in martial-arts training, or in yoga or dance, the skills are learned much more quickly and easily when broken down into a series of simple, easily mastered moves. Every Total Immersion student, novice to elite, begins by learning a series of positions that are extremely basic, yet establish a profound "connection" with the water. None of the positions is difficult. Yet mastering these simple moves in a logical progression can make such a powerful difference that within the first hour, you'll be flowing through the water with more ease and less effort than you ever thought possible.

As a beginning TI student, your hardest assignment may be developing the patience to slow down to **master the *art* of swimming, before you train for it as a *sport*.** Yes, those early, on-the-spot improvements are a thrill. But it's absolutely essential not to rush the program. Allow yourself to take as long as necessary to become completely comfortable with each of the simple movements we teach. For that 98-percent group in which most all of us find ourselves, piling on laps and more laps inevitably leads to struggle and more struggle as we fall back into old habits — certainly not the progress we had hoped for. But every swimmer who takes the time to first master the basic positions, and then the entire "form" or sequence of moves, will be able to swim with comfort no matter what, and will be able to advance through each of the more advanced skills with almost ridiculous ease and speed.

That's not a boast, it's a simple statement of fact. We've seen it happen with thousands of swimmers, regardless of their age, strength, physical condition, or level of coordination.

I hope you'll decide to join them.

Terry Laughlin
New Paltz, NY

Part 1

The Secrets of Fishlike Swimming

Chapter 1

How To Make Your Swimming Feel Good Again

So you want to become a better swimmer, but you're a bit bewildered by all the complicated and often conflicting advice on how to do that? Well, you have plenty of company. Welcome to what I call The Great Paradox of Swimming: One of the most popular fitness sports is also one of the most frustrating.

The popularity of swimming is well documented. Fitness surveys regularly place it among the top three choices along with walking and running. And why not? It's aerobic for healthful conditioning, it's nearly weightless for injury prevention, it works all the major muscle groups for completeness, and it's suitable for people of all ages throughout their lifetimes. It's also a necessary safety skill for anyone on or around the water. On top of all that, it's comfortable on both the hottest and coldest days of the year, since a pool is a controlled environment.

But swimming's frustration factor is also well documented. For unlike running and walking, which most people can do efficiently and effectively without instruction or practice, swimming well takes lots of both. In fact, as ideal as swimming is for health and fitness, only a tiny fraction of the population can swim well enough to enjoy *all* of its benefits. Both the American Swimming Coaches Association and the National Swim School Association estimate that only two of every 100 Americans are able to swim well enough to complete even a quarter mile without stopping. Thousands who can run mile after effortless mile find themselves panting and exhausted after just a few laps in the pool. "How can this be," they wonder, "since I'm in such good shape?" Lacking an answer, too many simply towel off, get dressed, and walk out of the pool forever, losing the opportunity for a lifetime of effective conditioning and steady improvement.

Swimming can frustrate even experienced athletes who can comfortably swim a mile or more, but who have trained religiously for years without much progress. Many have sought help, only to receive instruction that produces no lasting improvement. Many of these athletes eventually perceive swimming to be so complicated and mysterious that they don't know *what* to work on, or how to work on it. A dedicated swimmer can easily receive hundreds of "stroke tips" over the course of several years, each tip focused on different aspects of the stroke, many tips in outright conflict with each other, and all given with equal emphasis. So when improvement does occur, it's often fleeting and hard to reproduce.

And just in case drowning you in stroke technicalities doesn't take all the fun out of the sport, there are always the aquatic drill sergeants to remind you that swimming must also be *hard work*. Coaches and competitive swimmers embrace a boot-camp belief that only grueling and agonizing training will enable you to swim your very best, and few ever question this philosophy. The unfortunate result? Years of competitive swim training degrade an activity that many of us first experienced as joyful play into tiresome drudgery. Small wonder so many competitive swimmers are relieved to "retire" in their early teens.

That was my story. As a kid I spent most of my summers playing baseball or basketball each morning, and "playing" at swimming each afternoon. In the pool I was weightless and free, and it fast became my favorite playground. By exploring what I could do in water that wasn't possible on land, I learned spontaneously how to move easily through water. I may not have been terribly efficient or fast, but being completely comfortable and confident in the water was a great starting point.

The best part of that experience ended abruptly at age 15 when I joined a swim team. Now I had a coach to tell me the "right" way to swim, and warn me that I would have to work very hard to improve. I enjoyed hard work then as I do now, so I loved testing myself in workouts and meets and did well as a distance swimmer. But in the process I also lost the pure joy of being weightless and free in the water. I was way too busy pushing through pain barriers and thousands of laps to have any fun, and when I reached 21, I realized swimming had long ago become a chore, and happily retired.

But I never got over what I'd lost, and as I began coaching others and "learned from their learning," I began to see ways to make swimming — theirs *and* mine — pleasurable and satisfying again. It took until my late 30s, after 17 years away from traditional training and competition and free to spend my pool time exactly as I wanted, to rediscover the intensely satisfying, sensual side of swimming well, and to use that style of swimming to become fit, and fast.

Ten years later, my regular swim training is still mainly focused on doing what feels best. And I've discovered to my great happiness that doing what *feels* best also helps me *swim* the best. Never before has swimming been this satisfying. *Every* pool session is enjoyable, stimulating, and interesting. *Every* stroke I take feels smoother, more effortless, more in harmony with the water than did the millions of yards I thrashed out in college 30 years ago. I have seen my stroke efficiency, and my understanding of what works to increase it, grow without interruption for 10 years.

If continuing to improve into your 40s and beyond in a sport as "frustrating" as swimming seems too good to be true, remember this: Swimming integrates so many subtle skills that you can continue making new discoveries for years and years. That's why I consciously swim in a way that is *designed* to produce greater awareness. Like you, I'm motivated to increase my mastery of the sport and also like you — I hope — I expect to continue to get great pleasure and satisfaction from my swimming for decades to come.

My own story of burning out on the "old way" before coming to my senses and seeing the "new way," explains why the Total Immersion system enjoys such an enthusiastic following. Thousands of swimmers have found that TI has a solution for nearly every frustrating experience they've ever had in swimming. We explain the challenges and common problems of swimming in a simple way that makes sense. We've developed solutions to most of those common problems that anyone can understand and use without any advanced training. We've made the path to efficient swimming clear enough that swimmers can now confidently practice in a way that they know will really make a difference. In doing that, we've unlocked the secret of continuous improvement and showed how to accelerate that improvement. And, finally, we've replaced boring workouts with purposeful, interesting, and engaging *practice*.

The result is a style of swimming that, among its many virtues, *always feels good*. It looks good, too. Fluent and graceful TI swimmers are instantly recognizable to a growing number of other swimmers. Whether it's a 70-plus fitness swimmer flowing so effortlessly up and down the pool that strangers stop to ask whether he or she is "swimming TI," or whether it's an entire team of age groupers that has been coached "the TI way," our alumni are in a class by themselves.

Simple Grace: How To Swim Better in Four Easy Steps

The reason our TI methods work as fast as they do is simple: They've had to. By teaching hundreds of workshops that last just a weekend, rather than giving lessons that go on for weeks — that is, by having *hours* to teach fluency, not months or even years as most coaches have — we've been forced to develop a teaching approach that virtually eliminates wasted time or effort. And since so many of our students are relatively inexperienced, we've done away with all of the technical mumbo-jumbo that sometimes seems to be the pride of other coaches. Our instruction is uniformly simple and understandable. In the process of all this, we've found it doesn't have to take a long time to learn the basics of good swimming. In fact, the key to learning to swim with almost ridiculous ease comes down to just four basic steps:

1. Learn to be in *harmony* with the water. Water is an unnatural and, for many of us, a threatening environment. Our bodies were not designed to travel easily through it (how well we know!), and our basic swimming instincts cause us to fight it, not work with it. We naturally become models of inefficiency, filled with tension and so inhibited we can't possibly move freely. Bad all around. For when we don't move freely we certainly don't flow, and since water is a fluid, flowing freely through it is the very definition of efficiency.

Happily, one skill pretty much automatically puts you in harmony with the water: balance. When you learn balance first, you not only stop fighting the water and wasting energy, but also learn comfort and ease, which allows you to master every other swimming skill much faster.

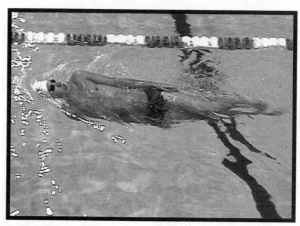

Step #1 for Fishlike Swimming: Learn to be effortlessly balanced in the water.

2. Learn to *rotate* your core body rhythmically, fluidly, and effortlessly. Lacking arms and legs, fish propel themselves through the water by oscillating or undulating their bodies — economical, incredibly powerful, and utterly effortless. Whether cruising lazily or darting with blinding speed, fish never seem to be *trying*. In fact they're *not* trying, at least not by our standards, because that effortlessness is produced by core-based propulsion, and core-based propulsion is enormously efficient.

In "human swimming," propulsion instinctively comes from churning the arms and legs. To speed up, you churn them harder and faster. What that does best is make waves and create turbulence. It's also exhausting. What churning and a fast turnover don't do is produce effective propulsion. For your swimming to be powerful and effortless, your movements should originate in the core (trunk) of the body, not in the arms and legs. Your movements should also be rhythmic. Fishlike swimmers learn rhythmic, coordinated core-body movement: body rolling or rotation for freestyle and backstroke, undulation for breaststroke and butterfly. Those core-body rhythms release the energy, power, and movement rhythms that subsequently become a strong, comfortable swimming stroke.

Long-axis rotation is the key to fluent freestyle and backstroke.

Short-axis rotation is the key to fluent butterfly and breaststroke.

3. Learn the most *slippery* body positions. Water is thick. Drag is what makes you slow, and tired. There is no workout or training program that can ever help you win the battle with drag. But you can learn to avoid it. Torpedoes, submarines, and racing boats are all sleekly shaped for the same reason fish and aquatic mammals are: so they can be slippery, moving through the water as fast as possible with the least waste in effort or power. Because drag increases exponentially as speed goes up (twice the speed, *four* times the drag), drag reduction pays off exponentially as speed increases. That's why humans who learn to maintain shapes and positions that are far more slippery than their old way of swimming see such a rapid and dramatic improvement. Slippery swimmers — like torpedoes and boats — need far less power or effort to swim at any speed.

4. Link the *propulsive actions* of your arms and legs to your core-body rhythms. Learning to pull and kick happens very early in the "Human Swimming" lesson plan. That's OK, as in Red Cross instruction, when the objective is to keep people safe by teaching them how to simply stay afloat and move toward safety. But it's not OK when the goal is efficient swimming, and it's an unfortunately common strategy. Even swim coaches, teaching technique to more advanced students, define "technique" as "how to use your hands to push water toward your feet."

In the TI approach, focus on the propelling actions comes at the end. First you learn to have a long, balanced, and effortlessly rotating core body. Only then do you link arm and leg movements to the body's rhythms. This provides effortless power and ensures that your swimming will be fluent and graceful.

But again, none of these shapes or positions is natural or instinctive, nor are the skills of balance or body roll. They must be learned. And with the help of the clear and logical course of instruction in the chapters that follow, they can be learned by anyone.

Chapter 2
Stroke Length:
The Secret to Becoming a Better Swimmer

Good swimmers have one thing in common: They make it look *easy*. Genuinely great swimmers – and there may be only a handful of them in the entire world – are so fishlike that they look downright *elegant*, in the same way that Michael Jordan looked elegant playing basketball. Genuinely great swimmers look so graceful and controlled that you'd never suspect they were going all out.

What has that to do with the rest of us? Everything. I have found it is possible – with a lot of coaching experience and with my eyes wide open – to understand what great form is all about, and then to pass along the secrets to other swimmers. Certainly I've learned more about what to teach and how to teach it by watching truly gifted swimmers than I've learned from reading books about swimming.

But the revelations didn't come overnight. Even in high school and college, when I was definitely *not* the kind of swimmer anyone would describe as "gifted," I was fascinated by teammates who could swim faster than I could while looking as if they were loafing along at half speed. So I made it my business to understand how they did what they did. Now, after more than 30 years of swimming and coaching – and watching – I can well understand the excitement of Ted Isbell, a TI disciple who coaches the Channel Islands Aquatic Club in Ventura, CA. After observing the fastest teenage backstroker in the world, Aaron Peirsol of the Irvine (CA) Novas Swim Team, Ted wrote to me about what he'd witnessed:

"My older son competes against Aaron so I've had many opportunities to watch him swim. I've counted Aaron's strokes per lap many times and although he's always the fastest swimmer in his age group, he consistently takes 25 percent fewer strokes than other swimmers. In fact, if you cup your hands around your eyes to isolate Aaron during a race, you'd think he'd be in last place because he appears to be swimming in a leisurely fashion. If you shift your 'tunnel' view to the second swimmer (usually 10 to 15 yards behind Aaron), he appears to be swimming hard enough to break a world record. As you remove your hands from your eyes, you are stunned by the lead that Aaron has gained, swimming so effortlessly."

And that's the key. Peirsol, as is often true of the world's best swimmers, has the rare ability to swim at top speed on far fewer strokes per lap than his peers, making fast swimming look effortless. Most of the rest of us, on the other hand, can make even slow swimming look like struggle. The better the swimmer, the less struggle you'll see as they move through the water...and the more they'll look like Aaron Peirsol.

Among recent world-class swimmers, Alexander Popov is my favorite example. Popov has admittedly been blessed with great athletic talent, but his coach, Gennadi Touretski, has also made a very conscious effort to teach and reinforce fluidity and relaxation and make them habitual in Popov's swimming.

The impression I get from Aaron Peirsol, from world-class champions such as Alexander Popov, and from virtually all exceptionally "fishlike" swimmers, is that they always seem to be *of* the water, not just *in* it. The word that best captures the quality of their swimming is "flow."

And what is the secret to flow? For years I was convinced it was pure talent. Great swimmers, I believed, somehow knew *in their bones* how to remain fluid and relaxed when they were swimming fast. The rest of us could just watch in envy. But after 10 years of intensive teaching, I now realize that fluid and relaxed swimming is possible for anyone who pursues it logically and analytically. Using simple information, you can understand exactly how flow is achieved and then, to a surprising degree, go on to actually achieve it for yourself.

Once you've "broken the code" of fluid, relaxed swimming, you can consciously practice, just as Alex Popov does, the movements and qualities that produce it, and that all but guarantee you'll swim your best. Not that you'll swim as well or as fast as an Aaron Peirsol, but you will swim as well and as fast as *you* are capable of swimming.

And the secret is precisely what Ted Isbell noticed when watching Peirsol: a longer stroke. The technical term is stroke length (SL). This secret is actually widely known, but for some reason that I can't comprehend, nearly all coaches and swimmers ignore it. Makes as much sense as knowing a simple shortcut to solving a tough math problem, and stubbornly insisting on solving it via the long, involved method — then getting the wrong answer anyway! Coaches and swimmers alike are conditioned to pursue success mainly through sheer sweat. More and harder laps are how they assume they'll get faster, even though more and harder laps actually tend to make your stroke shorter, not longer. Hard work, done without sufficient care and thought, can actually *slow* a swimmer's progress.

An even more powerful impediment than habit is instinct. Most every swimmer in the world who wants to go faster automatically thinks first of churning the arms faster. And a faster stroke (*i.e.*, higher stroke rate, or SR) results in a *shorter* stroke — again, just the ticket for swimming slower, instead.

Stroke Length: The Mark of Champions

How do we know stroke length is so important? It's a fair question, and easily answered. Over the last 20 years, curious scientists with time on their hands have attempted to discover if the secret to fast swimming could be reduced to some identifiable common factor. In several independent studies, these researchers analyzed the results of important swim meets and, aided by videotape or direct, personal observation, tried to figure out what made the faster swimmers faster. Each study produced the same result: Winners took fewer strokes. In general, the fewer strokes each subject took, the faster he or she swam. And that proved true not just for the champions, but all through the ranks.

More compelling still, when researchers cast a wider net to analyze the results of several Olympics, and of every US Olympic Trials from 1976 to 1996, and even of lesser meets such as the 1998 Iowa State High School Championships, this increasingly open "secret" was consistently evident in nearly all events. In fact, you can test it yourself at any local meet. Count strokes per length for swimmers in the slower heats of nearly any event, and compare their counts with the swimmers in the faster heats. The faster swimmers will almost certainly take fewer strokes.

This simple insight has incredible potential to transform your own swimming, if you'll just use it. But, as I said, few swimmers or their coaches do use it. Most continue to train as if the pace clock and the yardage total were all that mattered. If these studies had identified aerobic power as the key to better swimming, that intense focus on distance, time, and effort would logically seem to be the most effective training tool. Yet not one of the studies concluded that.

None of this is to suggest that fitness is unimportant. But at the Olympic Trials and at the Olympics themselves, *everyone* has worked hard; *everyone* is at peak fitness. Yet certain swimmers still have an edge over all the others. And that edge, it turns out, is a longer stroke. Plenty of athletes pump iron or muscle their way through endless laps with huge paddles and/or drag suits, as if sheer strength was the surest way to swim faster. Yet when scientists study the impact of strength on swimming, they usually find that the best swimmers in the world are *less* powerful than any number of mediocre swimmers. So weight-room visits and power-training swim sets aren't the answer.

Meanwhile, Ted Isbell and a growing number of "evolving-paradigm" coaches (as TI advocates like to call themselves) across the US have made SL the central focus of their training. With what results? All of these coaches report dramatic, even unprecedented, improvements. The proof, to paraphrase, is obviously in the pool.

What, Exactly, *Is* Stroke Length?

To work effectively on your SL, you'll need to understand what it is. Stroke Length, in fact, is one of the least understood terms in swimming (for simplicity, I'll refer to it as SL, and to stroke *count* per length of the pool as s/l). Even though swimmers are beginning to catch on that a long stroke is advantageous, most are still unsure of exactly what stroke length means or how to make a stroke longer. Do you do it by reaching farther before your hand goes in? Or by pushing the water farther toward your feet?

Most swimmers do, in fact, think of SL as "how far you reach forward and push back with your hand." Coaches, on the other hand, understand that there's more to SL than just "the length of your reach and your push," but they seldom know how to directly and significantly improve it. When I eavesdrop as a visitor during practices, I hear directives from the deck such as, "You've got to make your stroke longer!" which the swimmer naturally interprets as "Reach farther forward and push back more." This will result in a small increase in SL, but in most cases (the 98% of us who are not intuitive swimming geniuses), that increase will not last for very long. It will, in fact, be lost the moment the swimmer tries to go faster. Nor will it bring the swimmer anywhere near his or her best possible SL. So the swimmer remains unconvinced and goes back to relying on SR (stroke rate) for speed.

Just as trying to reach farther forward and push farther back has little effect on SL, a swimmer's limb length isn't the critical factor either — though you'd never know it from the staff at the Olympic Training Center. At the OTC, I've watched coaches and researchers measure a swimmer's reach (touch as high as possible on the wall, mark the spot; let the hand hang down at the side, mark the spot; measure the distance between the two marks) in an attempt to predict optimal SL. Yes, a swimmer's reach will have *some* influence on the SL he or she can achieve, but not as much as you'd think.

How do I know? Because I've worked for years on my own SL, not to mention the SLs of thousands of students who have attended TI workshops. I've seen countless swimmers of below-average height (and modest reach) who have *looked* much "taller" in the water than swimmers who were, in fact, tall on land (with much greater reach). These shorter swimmers turned out to have a much greater SL as measured by their s/l (strokes per length of the pool).

This discrepancy baffled me for years, as I struggled to increase my SL without much success. So long as I worked on it in the ordinary way, by trying to reach more and push back more, I managed to increase it by a puny 5% each year or two. Then my teaching experiences began showing me the importance of being balanced and slippery, and all at once I was able to boost my SL by astonishing amounts — 20% in just a few weeks — and to help other swimmers score SL improvements of 10% to 50% literally overnight. Often, these were people who knew the value of SL and had been trying for years to improve theirs by doing a better job of pushing water toward their feet. It hadn't worked.

The reason stroke length doesn't have a lot to do with arm length, or with how far you reach forward and push back, is because SL is *how far your body travels each time you take a stroke.* So it's mostly your body position – not your height or strength or the length of your arms – that affects the distance you will travel on each stroke. The best way to measure your SL is simply to make a habit of counting strokes — at all speeds, and on virtually every length you swim. You'll soon find there's not a single number that represents your "best" stroke count. Rather, you'll discover you have a stroke-count *range* — fewer on shorter repeats and/or when you're swimming slower; more when you're going farther or faster. Your primary goal during much of your swim training should be twofold: Gradually lower that entire range; and reduce the difference between its upper and lower end. At other times, you'll just maintain a consistent stroke count and work at developing more speed at that count.

But be warned: Not everyone agrees on which strokes count for "stroke count," and which don't. Purist coaches and researchers insist on measuring SL only between the flags, to factor out the glide (*i.e.*, non-stroking time) that occurs on turns and pushoffs. For reasons I'll explain later, I prefer the far simpler measure of counting all strokes (hand hits). If you take fewer strokes to swim a given distance, you've improved your SL. Period. All that really matters is whether you're spending your precious pool time concentrating on things that will help you swim faster or more easily, and counting strokes does exactly that. A "pure" SL number is important only to researchers who may need exact SLs in order to compare one swimmer to another. The swimmer you most need to compare yourself to is *you*. If your range was 17 to 24 s/l last year and 14 to 20 this year (or if you can swim faster at each point in that 17-to-24 range), stay the course; you're doing something right.

What, Precisely, Can Better SL Do for Me?

The key to becoming a better swimmer can be found in a simple equation:

$$V = SL \times SR$$

or Velocity equals Stroke Length multiplied by Stroke Rate. How fast you swim (V) is a product of how far you travel on each stroke (SL), multiplied by how fast you take those strokes (SR). In that way, at least, swimming is no different from running or in-line skating or cross-country skiing, where the equivalent terms would be Stride Length and Stride Rate.

Throughout most of the animal kingdom, the really fast creatures — race horses, greyhounds, cheetahs — use about the same stride rate at all galloping speeds. So do most really fast humans, such as Marion Jones and Michael Johnson. They run faster by taking *longer* strides, not by taking them faster. It's only when humans get into the water that we suffer a form of momentary biomechanical derangement, resorting to churning our arms madly when we want more speed.

It seems self-evident that a longer stroke or stride would be more efficient than a shorter one, but in the water a longer stroke is *much* more efficient. Here's why. First, there's the energy cost of a higher SR. As you increase SR, the energy cost goes up by a *cube* of that increase. Double your stroke rate and you burn energy eight (2 x 2 x 2) times faster. Second, there's the effect of a higher SR (and the higher heart rate that unavoidably accompanies it) on your coordination. As SR increases, your ability to stay coordinated, fluent, and efficient diminishes rapidly. As your form becomes more ragged and inefficient, the energy cost goes up even more. And, finally, you disturb the water around you far more when you're churning than when you're gliding smoothly. In essence, a fast turnover is like constantly swimming in white water. Your hand can't "grip" churned-up water nearly so well as it grips still water, and one of the surest ways to find more still water to grip is to swim with a greater SL and lower SR.

If we plug some simple numbers into our formula $V = SL \times SR$, we can clearly see the advantages of an improved SL. Let's say two swimmers racing 200 yards both pass 100 yards in 60 seconds. But swimmer "A" took 60 strokes (an SR of 30 cycles/minute) while swimmer "B" took only 54 strokes (an SR of 27 cycles/minute). Swimmer "A" will have "spent" far more heartbeats to swim the first 100 than swimmer "B," who will have more heartbeats remaining "in the bank" to win the race. If both swimmers have an effective SR "ceiling" of, say, 32 cycles/minute, swimmer "B" can potentially raise his SR — and speed — far more to unleash a powerful finishing sprint. By learning to swim the first half of the race in fewer, longer strokes, swimmer "B" has increased the range of strategies he can employ to win a tight race.

What Makes My SL Go Up or Down?

Although you're usually not aware of it, virtually everything that happens in practice influences your SL in some way — the distance of your repeats, how much you rest between them, the length of your sets, how fast you're swimming, your heart rate. But the single most important reason for a mediocre SL is *failure to pay attention to it.* If you are not consciously monitoring how your SL is holding up at various speeds and distances, your instincts will successfully tempt you to fall back too much on SR. Let's consider what you can do today to raise your SL to its optimal level.

SL can be improved in two ways. The easiest way is to minimize drag, and you do this by simply *repositioning* your body in the water to make yourself *more slippery.* The effect is that your body goes farther, with more ease and less deceleration, on a given amount of propulsion. The other way to improve SL is to maximize propulsion, and you do this by focusing on doing a better job of *moving your body forward.*

When I began teaching TI workshops in 1989, swimming technique was about one thing: how you use your hands to push water toward your feet.

Every coaching clinic, talk, or article on improving your swimming focused on pushing water toward your feet more effectively, and most swimming research centered on it. Swimmers themselves thought of little else. All emphasis was on maximizing propulsion rather than on minimizing drag.

But thinking about swimming was on the verge of a sea change. I had recently become acquainted with an independent thinker named Bill Boomer, who urged coaches to at least balance their emphasis on teaching propulsion skills with some attention to teaching swimmers how to minimize drag. Like most coaches, I had focused on teaching swimmers to propel themselves better and, because my interest in technique and teaching had always been so acute, I had become more adept than most at it. As I began to understand more and more the wisdom of Boomer's approach, I realized there was an enormous amount of information on how to teach propulsion, but next to nothing on how to teach slipperiness — eliminating not just drag but also the number of heartbeats a swimmer would routinely have to "spend."

So having already shifted my full-time preoccupation from *giving workouts* (teaching propulsion) to *teaching technique*, I decided to divide my energies between showing people how to propel themselves better — which I could already do very well — and teaching them how to be more slippery, a process that was still very much an art, and a highly experimental art at that. I was clear on one thing: I was going to measure my success as a teacher by how much my students improved their SL. And, right from the start, I noticed a striking phenomenon with *every* student. When I was successful in teaching them how to push water toward their feet, I would see a modest improvement in their SL. When I was successful in teaching them to become more slippery and to do a better job of eliminating drag, I would see a *dramatic* improvement in their SL. That got my attention in a hurry, and we soon began to devote more and more of our precious pool time to "slippery swimming."

Over the past 10 years, we've helped thousands of "average" swimmers learn to be more fishlike in the water. We've had a limited amount of time to work with each of them – two days (five days for kids) isn't much time to unlearn a lifetime of bad habits *and* to imprint something new. So we've had to refine and be highly selective about *what* we teach and *how* we teach it. The result is that we've looked for what really matters in teaching each of the four strokes, and we've developed what we feel is an unbeatable system for teaching. So let's begin learning how to be more slippery in each of the strokes.

Balance:
Becoming Fishlike Starts Here

"For a person to learn to maintain balance while walking normally, a certain amount of time and repetition are needed. Moreover, that repetition needs to be pretty much just walking normally.

"Now for a person to maintain balance while break-dancing on a trotting horse's back (I took my kid to the circus last week), to avoid falling down and getting trampled by the elephant next in line, a great deal more time and repetition are needed. And that repetition needs to be pretty much just break-dancing on a horse's back, or selected pieces of that skill ordered in a progressive manner, so as to end up with something people will pay to see.

"My sense is that swimming is more like break-dancing on a horse's back than walking. Whenever we do anything in the water, the neuromuscular system is inextricably drawn to the 'wrong' conclusions about what balance is and how to achieve it. Not wrong for land-based activity—wrong for water-based activity." —TI Senior Coach Emmett Hines

"Since your workshop last week, I've been swimming twice a day. The reason is, I'm afraid if I wait too long I'll have forgotten how to be balanced in the water. Every time I get in I hope to myself, 'please, please, feel like it did last time.' I've never felt anything like it! I can swim at my usual pace, yet I feel like I'm literally just floating along." —a TI workshop alumnus

Sad to say, but poor balance will limit, or at least slow, the progress of probably 98% of all swimmers—*even though it's among the simplest of all skills to teach*. In fact, though few people seem to realize it, poor balance is why "human swimming" so often seems frustrating and difficult.

Our balance *in* water is not much better than it is *on* frozen water. The primary reason we don't catch on to this is that the painful penalty for losing our balance on an icy surface keeps us *highly* attuned to being careful and paying attention, but in the water there's no danger of broken bones or other impact injuries from poor balance. And because virtually all swimmers are unbalanced from the time they take their first strokes, most of us simply assume that's how swimming is *supposed* to feel. So we go on to more and harder laps, figuring the way to deal with how tired we get is still *more* laps, and all the while burning our unbalanced stroke into muscle memory. Only when we finally learn balance, real balance, do we realize how much easier swimming can be.

That's why mastering balance is the bedrock, non-negotiable foundation of "fishlike" swimming, a step that must be taken by every would-be swimmer before *anything* more advanced is attempted. In that sense, our swimmers are no different from the pre-toddler taking her first uncertain steps. Developing the dynamic balance that will transform walking from a near-impossible task to a no-brainer may take months of practice, but that ability starts a process that will later enable every movement/navigation skill imaginable, from running and bicycling in the pre-school years, to rehearsed movements such as ballet in toe shoes, and ultimately to split-second balance skills used in such sports as soccer and downhill skiing.

In each instance the body's center of gravity (several inches below the navel) must artfully be kept aligned over the feet while the body is moving in ways that want to upset that alignment. We spend virtually all day, every day of our lives, consciously or unconsciously refining or practicing some form of that skill. And our motivation to excel at balance on land is great for if we don't, we'll be terrible at sports or at least could fall down a lot and fracture things.

Fast forward our toddler maybe six years, and see her join the swim team. Now she is working to master a dramatically different balance skill — trying to stay horizontal in water — while her body is still faithfully trying to keep its center of gravity over her feet, the worst possible thing for her swimming. Fortunately, learning this new balance skill is much simpler. Over the next few years in the water, she will need to master only two basic forms of balance: one for the long-axis rotation used in freestyle and backstroke, the other for the short-axis undulation of butterfly and breaststroke. And the better and faster she learns them, the more likely she'll become a really successful swimmer. In fact, it's likely that *no other skill* will have a greater influence on her swimming progress. Balance is *the* essential ingredient of fluent swimming.

Unfortunately, it's also the ingredient least likely to be developed because virtually no one — swimmers, teachers, or coaches — fully grasps it. If our student is learning in a Red Cross class, it's a virtual lock that her instructor will be clueless because balance isn't even mentioned in Red Cross instructor-training materials. If she's learning on a swim team, she can expect her novice coach to possibly pay lip service to the idea ("Balance? Oh yeah, it's that pushing-the-chest thing."), then two minutes later reverse himself and declare, "You've got to kick harder to keep your hips up." And that will be only the most common of a multitude of energy-wasting compensations she will learn to employ because she hasn't truly mastered balance.

The Myth of the "Weak Kick"

Whenever I hear a swimmer bemoaning her weak kick, I remember how my introduction to in-line skating convinced me I had a weak back. I took up "blading" because it looked like a fun way to work out. But it wasn't much fun at all the first time; after just 15 minutes, my lower back was so sore I had to quit. "That's odd," I thought. "My legs are doing all the work."

So I resolved to keep plugging away at this tough new workout until I'd whipped those apparently flabby back muscles into shape. But my very next time out, after a lot of looking around, I realized something: It was poor form, not weak muscles, that was making this activity so tough. The better skaters seemed fluid and effortless, moving with impressive speed simply by swaying from side to side. A smooth skater would lean all her weight on the left skate and then, *at just the right moment*, shift it all over to the right.

Others, probably like me, looked choppy and labored, and now I could see that the difference was not back or leg strength, but timing. Like all the other lurching skaters, my balance was off. My 200-pound body would teeter out too far, and those weary back muscles would have to snatch me back. Eventually, of course, they'd have gotten stronger, but then I'd merely have turned into a stronger bad skater instead of simply a bad one.

Most swimmers make the same mistake, but never realize it. They spend years trying to get stronger and fitter, when they could fix the real problem –

balance — almost overnight.

That's why we begin every TI workshop with a balance drill so simple that 90 percent of our students master it in 10 minutes, and it makes a huge impression every time. Though the drill teaches balance in a non-rolling position that we'll make little use of when we actually swim, the simple sensation of being fully supported by the water is a revelation to swimmers who have struggled for years without *ever* feeling very good. Ten minutes, and one simple skill, have made them feel more capable than anything else in their swimming experience so far. That's the power of balance.

We've taught this same basic drill to every level of swimmer from novice to world-class. All have learned something worthwhile from it. Even swimmers on the U.S. National Team have told me they could feel their hips seem to become lighter and higher, though we could not always *see* a striking difference. But with Olympic team berths and medals often decided by the tiniest of margins, even fractional improvements in efficiency can decide the race.

Their dramatic impact on *every* swimmer to whom we've taught our basic balance drills has shaped our TI instruction as nothing else has. Now in every camp, workshop, and swim lesson, as I said, we don't teach anything else until the pertinent balance skills have been mastered. And every one of the hundreds of coaches who have attended a TI workshop and seen how quickly a sense of balance can transform a struggling swimmer into a fluent one has gone home determined to teach balance — how it feels, how to achieve it, and how to maintain it.

What they have come to understand is that mastering balance is not only important in its own right, but also influences nearly every part of the stroke. Here's how.

1. Balance keeps you horizontal and slippery. Imagine kicking with a board angled slightly upward. Few swimmers would do that on purpose because the increased drag would make kicking a lot harder. Now imagine how much drag your whole body can create riding at a similar angle. If you're not perfectly horizontal, it's a *lot* more work to move yourself forward than if you are horizontal, but it's an obstacle many swimmers put in their own way. Over the past 10 years we've done underwater video analysis on more than 10,000 swimmers. Well over 90% – including a surprising number of elites — have had room to improve their balance, including many who appear from the deck to be doing fine.

Usually the best-hidden imbalance is the one that happens only momentarily during the stroke (*e.g.*, while breathing in freestyle). Viewed in slow motion or stop action from under water, it shows up glaringly. In fact, when you see it this way you have to marvel, "How did they ever swim fast like that?" The swimmer, of course, even the highly accomplished swimmer, usually has no idea this is going on at all *until* he does a simple drill — which we'll cover later — that finally alerts him to how much better it feels to be completely in balance.

2. Balance keeps you from wasting energy fighting "that sinking feeling." Let's clear up one thing right now: Your body is *supposed* to sink. Huge amounts of swimming energy are wasted because of the nearly universal misunderstanding that good body position means riding high in the water.

Novice swimmers seem to spend about 90 percent of their energy trying to keep from sinking because they think that if they do sink, they'll drown. This leaves little energy for moving forward.

And more accomplished swimmers — no longer in any danger of drowning — waste energy, too, because they've heard that good swimmers ride high on the water. Coaches sagely repeat it, and swimmers grimly try to do it. The reality? A sleek speedboat may begin to lift up out of the water and hydroplane at 35 or 40 mph, but a human body making 5 mph (world-record speed in the 100-meter free) will not. The pointless effort to stay on top not only squanders energy, but also keeps your arms and legs occupied, tremendously compromising their ability to propel you efficiently.

You save much more energy by *learning to sink in a horizontal position* instead of fighting to stay on top. As soon as you learn to find your most natural position in the water, you eliminate needless tension, you gain flow and ease, and you save energy for propulsion.

3. Balance "liberates your limbs" to propel you more efficiently. The technique-teaching style most coaches use is one I call "detect and correct." They observe a dropped elbow or splayed-leg kick and order, "Keep those elbows up!" or "Keep your legs closer together!" In nearly all cases, they're asking the swimmer to correct the symptom not the cause, much like a doctor instructing you to "Get that temperature down!" rather than seeking the cause of the fever.

Swimmers do have an instinctive understanding that it's desirable to remain horizontal and stable. When they sense themselves in a poor position, they automatically use their arms or legs to fix it. These compensating or stabilizing actions appear to the coach as stroke errors. As soon as the underlying balance error is corrected, in most cases, the more visible error corrects itself, too. The arms are freed up to perform their most valuable function — lengthening the bodyline and holding on to the water. The legs are freer to stay effortlessly in sync with core-body rotation. The stroke instantly becomes a far more efficient mechanism for propulsion.

4. Balance frees up more of your power. A baseball slugger's power is useless if he swings from an off-balance stance. A great in-line skater, cross-country skier, or speed skater's powerful quads can do no good if the body they're in isn't stable and ready for the push. A power lifter trying to heft hundreds of pounds overhead? Well, you get the idea. No good athlete ever attempts to perform in anything other than full dynamic balance. When you're on land, fully affected by gravity and needing *all* of your body's power to excel, your body just knows it can't deliver full power if it's not balanced.

In the water, it's different. Supported by buoyancy, your body weight is only 10% of what it is on land. And because you're not on solid ground, you're probably similarly restricted from using all of your potential power. On top of that, without those clear, dry-land signals, your body's balancing instincts can't work nearly as well to tell you how you're limiting — through poor balance — the in-water power you *do* have.

But limiting it you are. For a swimmer's power (as we'll explain later) comes from effortless core-body rotation, which unleashes the *kinetic chain* that ultimately powers the arms and legs. And as we have seen in countless thousands of unbalanced swimmers whose strokes we have studied on underwater video at TI workshops over the years, a swimmer who lacks dynamic balance loses the ability to freely rotate the body. In water, poor balance inhibits the full expression of power just as surely as it does on land. Many of these swimmers, vaguely aware that something is holding them back, think they should spend hour after hour building power with lat pulls and tricep presses. Truth is, they could free up effortless power instantly by improving their balance.

5. Balance frees you to be more fluent. Unbalanced swimmers, especially in freestyle, are often trapped in a cycle of frantic movement. They respond to the feeling of sinking by churning the arms more. The more they churn their arms, the shorter their strokes become (see the discussion on SL

in Chapter 2). The shorter their strokes become, the more strokes they have
to take to maintain speed. Eventually, they're flailing their arms frantically just
to keep moving.

As soon as they master balance, they escape the trap. They can move at
the same speed with a far more leisurely stroke, and can find a more natural
and fluent body rhythm.

How To Achieve Effortless Balance In Every Stroke

Our goal is to be "effortlessly horizontal" in the water. Note the key word
effortless. For if we accept the fact that the body constantly wants to get vertical in the water — good for keeping the head where it can breathe, bad for
swimming efficiency -- we can set about changing it relatively easily by using
the laws of physics, rather than our own sweat. We do this by nothing more
mysterious than correct positioning of body parts, and redistribution of body mass.

The process, of course, varies somewhat with the four strokes, though it
really comes down to just two types of balance: *continuous* balance as the
body rotates in the long-axis strokes of freestyle and backstroke, and *rhythmic re-balancing* within every cycle as the body undulates in the short-axis
strokes of breaststroke and butterfly.

The way to do it in both cases is fairly simple. First, keep your head in a
natural, neutral position — as close as possible to the way you hold it when
you're *not* swimming. And second, shift your body weight forward. "Press
your buoy," as I sometimes call the process of pushing down into the water
your normally buoyant chest cavity, until you feel as if you're being supported
by the water.

So let's examine how to stay balanced in any stroke.

Freestyle Balance: Getting Your Head in the Right Place

"Hide" your head. If you've read earlier Total Immersion books, you
know they stress the importance of achieving proper freestyle balance by leaning on your chest or "buoy." That's still an effective way to do it, but now that
I've had so many more opportunities to teach and observe swimmers learning balance, I've come to realize that for most of us, correcting head position
is actually more essential. In fact, simply getting the head in a neutral position
eliminates about 70% of the balance problems for people in our workshops.
So our teaching progression now starts with teaching them to "hide" the head,
then, once that is accomplished, to show them how to add just enough pres-

sure on the "buoy" to feel like the water is supporting them.

From the deck, it looks like this: The coaches know your head is in the right position when we can see no more than a sliver of the back of your head or cap visible above the surface any time you're looking down. From your point of view, it *feels* like this:

- a sense that a thin film of water could flow over the back of your head at any time
- a recognition that you're looking almost directly at the bottom between breaths, using only peripheral vision to see a bit forward
- a sense that you're leading with the top of your head, rather than with your nose
- a feeling that your hips and legs feel much lighter and are riding noticeably higher.

I want to be very clear about one thing: Hiding your head does not mean burying it under water. It also does not mean pressing your nose down. It does mean simply holding your head in a neutral position, the way you hold it when you're *not* swimming. When I'm coaching, as I look across the pool, I want to see that tiny sliver of the back of your head showing above the surface whenever you're not breathing. Or a thin film of water flowing over it.

Good balance starts with hiding your head.

Swim "downhill." We may no longer emphasize this as much as previously, but for many people – especially those "balance-challenged" folks who may be quite lean or have long legs (and particularly those with both) -- consciously shifting weight forward, constantly leaning on your chest, while swimming freestyle, remains very helpful. Hiding your head should make your balance *much* better, but if you still feel as if your hips and legs are sinking, then lean forward, too. How much? Press in until you feel the water pushing you back out. Whatever it takes to make you feel as if your hips are light, as if the water is simply carrying you. When that happens, you're experiencing the sensation we call "swimming downhill." You're not really, but the contrast with your prior battle to swim uphill makes it feel that way. Continue doing it very consciously until it starts to happen naturally. And this could take as much as six months of focused practice.

Press in until you feel as if you are swimming downhill.

Reach with a "weightless" arm. The best indicator that you are a truly balanced freestyler is the sensation of having a "weightless" arm. With poor balance, or a too-high head position, you have to use your arms to try to keep from sinking. The weight of your head and body drives them down as you try to reach forward. A balanced swimmer should be able to feel is if the extending arm is weightless, just floating effortlessly forward, until you *choose* to make your catch and begin stroking.

Use the fistglove® stroke trainer. One of the simplest and quickest ways to learn balance or make it more impeccable and natural is to wear fistglove® stroke trainers for 50 percent or more of your freestyle drilling and swimming. These black latex "mittens" tightly wrap your hand and make it impossible to use your arm as a support lever or to use muscle to swim. They force you to use your torso for balance and support and encourage you to use much more finesse while swimming. You'll soon find that a weightless arm is your only option. You can find more information about fistgloves at www.totalimmersion.net.

The fistglove® stroke trainer teaches balance and ease.

Breathing: Why Every Lungful Slows You Down

Breathing in freestyle, and trying to maintain impeccable balance at the same time, is the closest thing in swimming to coach Emmett Hines's earlier example of break-dancing on a horse's back. It is a lot to do all at the same time. The underwater videos of less-experienced swimmers at TI workshops, even swimmers who have some tentative sense of balance, all show the same thing: These swimmers may have some delicate equilibrium while looking down but as soon as they turn their heads to breathe, their balance falls apart. They are often shocked when we freeze the moment while studying the video. Is that really *their* body, so awkwardly contorted that it would seem impossible to maintain any forward momentum? Well yes, it is

This swimmer demonstrated good balance...until he took a breath.

Even when I've shot underwater video of elite swimmers, including one Olympic medalist, I've seen the effects of loss of balance during the breath. True, these effects are momentary and often so subtle that they cannot be seen from the surface. But they can't hide from the underwater video camera with its slow motion and freeze-frame functions. And it always looks the same. For a moment as the head turns, the swimmer shifts from using the arm to extend the bodyline or for propulsion, to using it for support. And in that moment — however brief — propelling efficiency is lost. Or, for a moment, the kick becomes subtly rushed. Or, just for a moment, the armstroke loses its connection with the "engine" of body roll. In every case, more energy is being burned.

Those momentary losses may be so subtle that they aren't even noticed by the swimmer, never mind by an observer up on deck. But they add up. If the swimmer breathes every stroke cycle, there will be 30 to 50 or more such moments of inefficiency in a race as brief as the 100-meter freestyle. And when Olympic gold medals can be lost by margins as slim as .01 second, such barely noticed breakdowns decide races.

How to Breathe with Balance Intact

The two most likely errors in freestyle breathing are (1) turning the head to breathe; and (2) lifting the head to breathe. Let's learn how to correct both.

The most efficient breathing movement comes from keeping your head on the head-spine line and connected to the core body. When you want to breathe, roll the body to where the air is. It might help to imagine that you're breathing with your bellybutton, rather than your mouth. Your head just goes along for the ride.

When you get this right, you should feel these sensations:

- Your *weightless* arm continues to glide forward as you breathe.
- Your body continues to slide through the water as you breathe.
- You can easily choose — with the barest minimum kick — to have more catch-up or overlap in your stroke, perhaps to practice *Front Quadrant Swimming* (see pages 40-43).

BREATHING *101*

Should I breathe to both sides?

One of the most common questions I get from swimmers is whether they should use alternate-side, or bilateral, breathing. This isn't strictly a balance issue, but as long as we're on the topic of freestyle breathing anyway, we may as well cover it.

The quick answer is yes, you should breathe to both sides. At least in practice. And on some occasions it can be an advantage while racing, too.

The primary reason is that it promotes more symmetry in the stroke: The goal is to make sure that whatever happens on one side of the body, happens the same way on the other side. Too often that's not the case, as I learned in a lesson about *habits* on my very first day of coaching in September 1972. It seemed that virtually my entire team of 15 college men at the US Merchant Marine Academy in Kings Point, NY, had lopsided freestyle strokes, rolling more to one side or the other and swinging wider on recovery on the same side. So the next day for warmup, I instructed them to swim 800 yards breathing to the "wrong" side. Instantly, every stroke in the pool was more symmetrical and balanced — the "blank slate" effect. Lacking a history of practicing bad habits, each swimmer's less-natural breathing side was actually more efficient.

Virtually all swimmers favor one side in breathing, and breathe to that side all the time because it feels better. Trying to breathe to the other side feels awkward, so you just don't do it. Who needs to feel even more awkward? The problem with breathing to only one side is that it tends, over time, to make your stroke lopsided and asymmetrical. And small wonder; In just an hour of swimming, you'll roll to your breathing side about 1,000 times, meaning all your torso muscles pull more in that direction and less to the other side. Multiply that by hundreds of hours of swimming and you can see how a lopsided stroke can easily become permanent.

Making a conscious decision in practice to breathe nearly as often on one side as the other has two benefits:

1. Using your more efficient, "blank slate" side more frequently will help your stroke overall, including your regular breathing side.

2. You'll have better command of a potential tactical racing advantage: In the pool you'll never have a "blind" side, and in open water you can check for landmarks wherever they may be, or avoid chop, or keep a rough swimmer alongside from splashing water into your face as you breathe.

The best way to get all these benefits is to practice bilateral breathing, which can be done in any number of ways. Awkward? Yes, that's how it feels at first to most everyone. But the awkwardness may be easier to deal with than you realize. Most TI workshop attendees come in as single-side breathers, but are able to comfortably breathe to either side by the time the workshop is over. The reason? They spend the entire weekend doing drills that teach bilateral balance and rolling — and breathing — to both sides. Regular practice of these drills virtually guarantees your awkwardness will soon be a thing of the past.

Once it is, you can be endlessly creative in your bilateral breathing patterns. And you'll want to be. For although breathing every third armstroke is the simplest, it also means you breathe one-third less often than when you're breathing every cycle to one side. On top of that, when you learn to lengthen your stroke, you will be getting still fewer breaths because you'll be taking fewer strokes per lap, so you may well feel unaccustomedly winded. Time to become more imaginative with your bilateral breathing pattern. Here are just a few options (assuming a swimmer who normally breathes to the left):

1. Breathe to your right side on one length and to your left on the next. That way you still get plenty of air, but develop a balanced stroke.

2. Breathe to your right side in warmups, cooldowns, and slower swimming sets, and to your left on main sets.

3. Breathe to your right side during the first few repeats of main sets, then shift gradually to your left side. Example: On a set of 5 x 100, breathe right on the first 100, 75 right/25 left on the second, 50/50 on the third, 25

right/75 left on the fourth, and breathe left on the fifth 100.
4. Experiment with 3L/3R or 4L/4R until you find a comfortable pattern.

Your goal, over the course of any week of swimming, is to breathe about as often to one side as to the other.

What About Breathing in Races?

When it comes time to race, many swimmers feel they must stick with the breathing patterns they've established in practice. This theory is fine for triathletes and open-water swimmers, who don't experience the air-deprivation of flip turns and may benefit from settling into a comfortable pattern of bilateral breathing. Pool racers, and sprinters in particular, however, need to take a more flexible approach. It is a good idea to breathe as little as possible in a 50. But you can't really "sprint" a 100, so it stands to reason that you need your air in order to produce the energy to swim it as fast as possible.

Sprinters have traditionally skipped breaths on the notion that every one makes you a bit slower. Well, if you can't fit the breath seamlessly into your stroke, it does. But if you can learn to sacrifice little or no speed with each breath, you'll gain a big advantage late in the race over those who do need to skip getting air in order to be fast. By breathing every cycle (except inside the flags) during the first 50, you might lose a tenth or two to someone who is breathing every two or fewer cycles. But as they're suffering aerobic distress on the final 50, you may gain back a full second. That strikes me as a pretty good trade.

Following that theory, sprinters can do two things:
1. Work constantly on developing a breathing form that doesn't interrupt balance, alignment, or rhythm. How? Not by taking fewer breaths, but by breathing *often*, and nearly the same number of times on both sides. Use the "blank slate" you have on your "non-breathing" side to help correct errors that have developed over the years on your breathing side.
2. Do a lot of sprint work in practice with an every-cycle breathing pattern, so that you learn to breathe without sacrificing speed. Remember: A fish-like swimmer can achieve cardiovascular benefits from breathing more - rather than less — frequently in practice.

Here are a couple of challenging breathing patterns that should work well for racers:
1. **Swim 8 x 75**. On each 75, breathe every 5 strokes on the first 25, every 3

strokes on the 2nd length, and every stroke (right-left-right-left) on the last length. Swim at a moderate pace. Focus on fitting in each breath smoothly and seamlessly. This will be easy on the first two lengths, and more of a challenge on the third. But if you can stay smooth and fluid while breathing every *stroke*, then breathing every *cycle* with no interruption in your flow should be easy.

2. **Swim 3 (or 4 or 5) x 200**. On each 200, use the following breathing pattern.
   - First 50: Breathe every 3 strokes.
   - Second 50: Breathe twice on the right, 3 strokes, then twice on the left.
   - Third 50: Breathe 3 times on the right, 3 strokes, then 3 times on the left.
   - Fourth 50: 4 breaths on right, 3 strokes, then 4 on the left.

This set allows you to practice a pure bilateral (same number of breaths on either side) pattern, but gives you more air the further you go into the set. Need more oxygen to maintain your pace and intensity as fatigue grows? You get more.

Backstroke Balance: Getting Hip to Body Roll

Here's my rule of thumb: If there's more than a fraction of an inch of water covering your hip bones in the backstroke, you need to improve your balance. Fortunately, learning balance in backstroke is usually easier than learning it in freestyle. For one thing, there's little risk that breathing will upset your balance. For another, there's a lot less temptation to fight your way back into equilibrium by using your arms because in the backstroke, the arms don't offer much leverage or support anyway. And even if they did, it's difficult to churn them rapidly the way out-of-balance freestyle swimmers are tempted to do. So, nearly everyone who swims backstroke often has *had* to learn some degree of balance in the torso. If they haven't, they've probably given up the stroke as just hopelessly awkward.

No need for anyone to give up. Virtually every swimmer can easily learn improved backstroke balance and, when you do, you'll find you expend far less energy on kicking.

"Hide" your head. Poor head position in backstroke is actually very common, and to some degree coaches and teachers are to blame. Tuck your chin into your throat and look slightly toward your feet while swimming, as you're usually advised, and you'll not only be uncomfortable but also set yourself up for neck and back tension, and cause your hips to sink dramatically, too.

Inexperienced swimmers, worried that water might come in the mouth or nose, most often tilt the head too far back, as if craning the neck, trying to keep the mouth as far as possible from the water. This position disconnects the head from the head-spine line, and also causes the hips to sink.

Both positions inhibit the swimmer's freedom to roll fully and effortlessly to both sides.

To understand the right head position, take your finger and trace a circle from an inch or so above your eyebrows (just below where your swim cap would be) down past the corner of your eye and high on your cheek (an inch or so inside your ear) under your jaw so it passes just under your chin and up the other side. The area inside this circle is all that should show above the surface while you kick, drill, or swim backstroke. One simple test is your ears — they should always be under water (see the illustrations on pages 100-101).

Next, adjust the angle of your chin. Hold your head so you could just fit an apple or your fist between your neck and chin. This gives you the most neutral and natural head position.

Finally, imagine you are carrying a glass of champagne on your forehead. Your head position should be so stable that you wouldn't upset the glass. It can be done. While teaching, I often ask swimmers to set their half-empty water bottle on their forehead and swim (or drill) a length of backstroke to help them gain a sense of how stable the head should be. With some practice, they become quite good at maintaining a stable head position. It really works.

Balance your torso. In backstroke, you "press your buoy" by leaning on your upper back (in a pressure band that runs from your sternum out toward your latissimus muscles on each side). Keep steady pressure on this band as you stroke and roll, and your hips will be lighter and higher in the water. As that happens, you'll spend less energy kicking.

Because all of this focus on maintaining dynamic balance will probably be new for you, it's a good idea to give it some concentrated practice. Spend time paying attention mainly to the sensation of leaning on your upper spine as you swim. You'll find it easier to learn what good balance feels like by practicing the long-axis balance drills described in Chapter 12 (and demonstrated on the video *FREESTYLE AND BACKSTROKE: The Total Immersion Way*). Knowing that feeling will, in turn, help you to apply this skill much faster. In any case when you *do* swim whole-stroke backstroke over the next few months, your balance will improve most dramatically if you shut out all distractions (like what you're doing with your hands) and think mainly about hiding your head and pressing in your upper back as you roll your whole torso — hips and shoulders together—rhythmically from side to side.

Breaststroke and Butterfly Balance: Rocking Your Way to Rhythm and Flow

In backstroke and freestyle, you balance by keeping your head in a neutral position and maintaining steady pressure on your buoy as your body rolls from side to side. In breaststroke and butterfly, the process is altogether different. Both of these short-axis strokes are *re*-balancing strokes.

In breaststroke and butterfly, the body rotates around the "short axis" (the line from hip to hip), producing an undulating motion. With each stroke and breath, the shoulders rise and the hips fall. As the body lengthens to full extension, the chest presses down, lifting the hips back up again. So you *give up* balance briefly as you begin each stroke, then regain it as you complete the stroke and lengthen the body.

This up-and-down rocking action provides several advantages:

1. It allows you to breathe with a minimum of head movement (very important, as we'll see later).

2. It produces maximum power with minimum work for both the pull and the kick, by recruiting torso muscles to drive the arms and legs.

3. It returns the body to its most streamlined, long-and-horizontal position during the gliding phase of each stroke.

Keep your head "in neutral." We've seen that a neutral head position is critical to balance in both of the long-axis strokes. It's just as critical — perhaps even more so — in breaststroke and butterfly. In fact, with countless swimmers I've observed, the simplest and quickest way to make an immediate, and often significant, difference in efficiency and speed in breaststroke and butterfly has been to simply get the head as close as possible to a neutral position while breathing. And between breaths, as well.

One way or another, head movement will always hurt your efficiency. Jutting the chin while breathing, excessively bobbing the head up and down, or moving your head independently of your body, can all have drastic effects on stroke length, the availability of power, and the effectiveness of the pull and kick in short-axis strokes.

The correction to excessive head movement in breast and fly is fairly simple. Just concentrate on the following:

1. Always look down slightly while breathing; you should see the water and not the far end of the pool.
2. Minimize head movement as you breathe; it can help to imagine you are wearing a neck brace.
3. Keep your head as close as possible to a neutral position at all times. This includes laying it between the arms — but *not* pushing it under water — as your arms reach full extension, following the breath.
4. Particularly in butterfly, practice a technique we call "taking a sneaky breath." Imagine someone is watching you swim. Try to "hide" your breath from them, making it difficult to tell whether you've taken one.

Press your buoy. A simple rocking motion — rhythmically pressing your sternum down, then releasing it to rock back up — is the essence of both butterfly and breaststroke. This motion is best learned by doing Short-Axis Pulsing (SAP) drills, also known as Body Dolphins, which we'll describe in Chapter 13. These drills can teach you not only to perform short-axis rotation rhythmically and effortlessly, but also to kick butterfly using an absolute minimum of energy. They can also help you learn to keep your head in a neutral position while breathing. If you've never worked on this before, I can guarantee that SAP drills are your fastest way to learn a more fishlike breast or fly.

The idea behind the drills is the same as the idea behind good whole-stroke swimming: to make rhythmic pulsing of the sternum one of the focal points. When you want to swim faster, avoid trying to pull or kick faster. Keep the focus primarily on your torso, and rock it up and down faster.

And again, as I suggested for backstroke, any swimmer who has never focused on short-axis pulsing will benefit from several months of blocking out thoughts of what the arms or legs are doing, freeing the brain to zero in on nothing more complicated than rocking your torso rhythmically.

Just as a balanced body fights the water less because of reduced resistance, the laws of physics also say that a longer body will slip through the water more easily than a shorter one. And happily, there are ways to make our bodies "longer," too — at least as far as the water is concerned. So now that we've gotten ourselves balanced, it's time to start "Swimming Taller."

Chapter 4

How To Swim Taller:
What Sleek Boats and Olympic Sprinters
Teach Us About Swimming

J ust like the other skills of Fishlike Swimming, "swimming taller" is neither natural nor instinctive for any but a handful of gifted athletes. But just as with those other skills, knowing how to make your body as long – from fingertips to toes — as possible in the water can be learned by anyone, given the right kind of practice.

The payoff for learning this skill is as dramatic as it is obvious — especially if you've ever watched the finals of the men's 100-meter freestyle (the race that decides the title of "world's fastest human") at the Olympics or World Championships. If you have, you may have noticed something striking about the finalists in those races: They look like they might make a pretty decent basketball team. In fact, all those who can swim 100 meters long-course freestyle in 49 seconds or faster seem to be about 6'5" (2 meters) or taller. The fastest women in the same events are usually 5'9" or taller. What gives?

Common sense suggests a couple of advantages taller swimmers might have. "Well, sprint races are usually decided by small margins," you might reason. "I suppose it helps to be taller so you can use your long arms to win those close touch-outs." Or, "It's probably an advantage to have long legs so you can turn a little farther from the wall." To some extent you'd be right, because such incremental advantages would unquestionably help you in a close race.

But the most significant swimming advantage to being taller is that the extra height makes your body into a longer boat or "vessel" in the water. And as any naval architect can tell you, longer boats are faster boats, other things being equal. A principle called Froude's Law says that as you increase the length of a vessel at the waterline, wave drag decreases. As wave drag decreases, less energy is wasted stirring up the water, so more is left to make the boat go forward. And though it may be a stretch to compare a 100-foot-long steel hull making 20 knots in open seas to a six-and-a-half-foot human trying to make two meters per second in a pool (and whose "vessel" is constantly shape-morphing with each stroke), there is no doubt swimmers can benefit greatly from trying to be more "Froude worthy."

Swimming researchers estimate the maximum speed of a human swimmer to be approximately one body length per second. So it's no surprise, in our example above, that swimmers who can swim faster than two meters per second (or faster than 50 seconds for 100 meters) do in fact tend to be at least two meters tall. All things being equal, this gives a 6'6" swimmer an advantage of approximately 10 yards in a one-minute race over a 6'0" swimmer. This explains why world-class sprinters look like basketball players...natural selection! (And what of those who are of only average height, say, 6 feet tall? They tend to be more successful in events where the winning time might be only 1.7 meters per second such as the men's 400-meter freestyle — or in short-axis events where the hydrodynamic laws give less advantage to the tall.)

Fortunately for those of us not endowed with unusual height — particularly those of us who have already stopped growing — there are several things we can do to maximize our speed potential by *swimming* taller without actually *growing* taller. And in the process, we might be able to take back the advantage from taller swimmers who don't know how to use their height to full advantage.

You swim taller mainly by rethinking how you use your arms. Our strongest instinct is to regard them as the paddles we use to push water toward our feet. "If I move forward by stroking," our logic goes, "I'll move faster by stroking faster." But stroking faster nearly always causes us to swim "shorter." We chop our strokes to speed them up. Not helpful. Instead, we must realize that the most important thing we can do with our arms is *use them to lengthen our vessel.*

It works like this. The most significant development as we go faster is that drag increases exponentially, meaning it takes a HUGE increase in power to swim faster if nothing else changes. But something else *can* change, and we can change it. Keeping your body line *as long as possible for as long as possible* during each stroke cycle is among the simplest things we can do to reduce drag. And anything we do to reduce drag hugely reduces the power required to swim at any speed.

Here's how you do it.

Swimming Taller in the Long-Axis Strokes
How to Eliminate Drag in Freestyle

1. **Hide your head and swim "downhill."** First things first. Keep working on these two balance aids until you feel a clear sense of a "weightless arm" before you actually start trying to swim taller. For if you haven't mastered balance and haven't learned to make the water support you, your arms will be so busy correcting balance that you won't be able to use them to lengthen your body.

Hide your head and swim "downhill."

2. **Lengthen your body with each stroke.** As you swim down the pool, instead of thinking "Stroke...Stroke...Stroke," think "Reach... Reach... *Reach.*" You'll still be stroking — the right arm strokes as the left arm reaches, and vice versa — but your focus will have shifted to the reaching arm. This will

change the entire focus of your swimming — from pushing water toward your feet (concentrating on what's happening *under* your body) to lengthening your body (concentrating on what's happening *in front of* your body). And that shift in focus will reduce your level of perceived effort. If you think of how it feels to put your arm into the sleeve of a jacket, you'll have it about right.

Use your hand to lengthen your body, not to push water toward your feet.

3. Reach *through*, not *over*, the water. Put your hand into the water fairly close to your head, just a few inches below the surface, then extend it forward. Reaching over the water is more natural, but a hand in the air is a weighted object that makes it more difficult to balance. Moreover, it does nothing to increase the length of your vessel at the waterline (remember Froude). But a hand extending just below the surface gives us that extra length. To get this right, practice this while doing your TI freestyle drills, and later while swimming: Imagine you are cutting a hole in the water with your hand and slip the rest of your arm cleanly through that hole.

4. Reach with a "weightless" arm. If all your brain cells are shouting "Reach!" as your hand enters the water, but your hand still stubbornly plunges toward the bottom as soon as it enters, there are two possible reasons: Either you haven't solved your balance problem (in which case, see #1), or the force of habit formed by millions of hurried or choppy strokes is still too powerful. If it's the latter, you may be able to correct it by a little creative self deception: Pretend each stroke is your last of the lap, and reach forward as if for the wall before you angle your hand down and *anchor* it (make it stand still as if holding an underwater rung) to begin the stroke. You're trying to form into a new habit the feeling of being able to extend your hand weightlessly, effortlessly, and unhurriedly before stroking, as if it was just floating out in front of you.

5. Use shoulder roll to extend your hand. Though you may feel as if your arm is weightless, you shouldn't feel as if it's disembodied. Just the opposite, in fact. Your arm is an extension of your core body, and it's body roll that drives one arm forward and the other one back. So make the most of it. You can work on this by extending each arm until you feel that shoulder touch your jaw. An added dividend: More body roll will add an inch or two to your reach — and to the length of your vessel. (See drill #2.1 on page 113 for more details.)

Rotate your body to get maximum extension of your hand.

6. Learn the "Switch," and practice Front-Quadrant Swimming (FQS). Swimming taller means you should always have one hand in front of your head — particularly at slower speeds, which also means that at some point in each stroke cycle *both* hands should be in front of your head. This is known as Front-Quadrant Swimming (FQS), though many people confuse it with catch-up swimming (a drill in which the recovering hand must touch the extended hand before stroking).

As the next illustration shows, our object is to learn to time strokes precisely so that one hand remains extended for slightly longer in each stroke, until the other hand is just about to enter the water. The quickest and easiest

way to learn this is with our series of "Switch" drills — Over Switch and Triple
Switch — which are described on pages 137-142, and which are shown on our
video *FREESTYLE AND BACKSTROKE: The Total Immersion Way.*

In Front-Quadrant Swimming, one hand is always in front of the
shoulders and being used to lengthen your bodyline.

7. Master one skill at a time. Swimming taller in freestyle involves far
more coordination of timing and fine-motor skills than it does in any other
stroke. So don't try to take on all six of our suggested stroke modifications at
once, unless you want to experience mental overload. Try to learn just one at
a time, in order. Since I've arranged them in the most logical sequence for
your central nervous system to absorb, mastery of one will lead naturally to
the next. Spend 10 to 20 minutes of each practice session on one skill, and
focus on only one or two skills in each session. If you allow yourself at least
two to three weeks to incorporate each skill, your learning process will go
much more smoothly.

A NOTE ON FRONT-QUADRANT SWIMMING

Front-Quadrant Swimming is by far our most controversial recommendation. Swimmers who practice FQS too rigorously can, in fact, find themselves restricted from reaching the stroke rates necessary to swim their fastest. To drive this point home, critics have pointed out that, at top speed, sprinters usually don't race with both hands in front of their head (though many of the fastest middle-distance and distance swimmers do). So let's pause briefly to clarify how to find out if FQS is really an advantageous strategy and, if it is, how to properly apply it in practice and in races.

In TI workshops and camps, we describe FQS as the most "negotiable" of all the skills we teach. Our advice is that all swimmers at least practice the Switch drills that teach FQS timing, enabling these swimmers to discover for themselves whether or not practice makes FQS feel comfortable and natural. A small percentage (less than 10%) of all the students I've worked with have found that FQS did in fact inhibit their natural sense of rhythm. The way around that for them, we discovered, was to use the Switch drills to add just a bit more *awareness* of length to their strokes without disrupting their natural rhythms in whole-stroke swimming.

For the great majority who can adopt FQS with a rhythm that feels comfortable, I explain that this is nonetheless still a *practice* strategy for imprinting timing that is not natural or instinctive. Do a good job of that by purposefully and consciously working on FQS at lower speeds in training, and on race day the nervous system will just know how to maintain the greatest efficiency at the highest rate. You'll be able to swim freely at the stroke rates and rhythms that move you fastest.

Skeptics counter that if FQS is so great, why doesn't Alexander Popov, one of the fastest humans in the water, bother with it? Glad you asked that. Because I can tell you that he does, having personally watched him for a cumulative total of several hours, both in meet warmup/warmdowns and in practice, while he was in New York for the 1998 Goodwill Games. Other coaches I know have also observed Popov's practices during his visits to the US, for anywhere from a couple of hours to three weeks. And we all observed the same thing: He swam most of his practice laps relatively slowly with impeccable form, and every stroke on those slower laps was done with considerable overlap — FQS timing.

The payoff always comes on race day when, as a result of this rigorous nervous-system training in practice, he maintains greater stroke length at his highest stroke rate than do swimmers who fail to practice FQS. That's also why he holds his form better in the closing stages of races, and finishes faster than other swimmers over the final 10 to 15 meters.

I wanted the sprinters I coached at West Point to be able to do that, too, so here's how we got the best out of FQS while avoiding its possible pitfalls: At super-slow paces, we consciously practice the greatest degree of overlap or FQS timing. As the pace increases, we give up overlap bit by bit, trying to hold on to as much as possible without feeling restricted. As we close in on race pace and race tempo, we just do what feels most natural. As a distance freestyler myself, I use exactly the same approach in my own training.

Yes, there are times when we end up sacrificing more stroke length than we'd like in the bargain, but we don't get down on ourselves about it. We simply make a note to remember how it all felt, and continue to do purposeful nervous-system training at all lower speeds, learning to better negotiate the trade-off of SL for speed.

The results, over the course of each six-month season during my three years coaching at West Point, have been undeniable: a significant improvement in the SL my swimmers can maintain at their highest speeds. And by season's end they can invariably swim *significantly* faster, and with significantly improved SL.

I can tell you from personal experience that it doesn't just work for the youngest and fastest among us, either. Over several years of practice, I've been able to gradually improve my speed at every stroke count (13 s/l, 14 s/l, etc.) and have dropped my stroke count per 25 yards in races from 19-20 to 16-17. This in turn has made me feel much more smooth and controlled at my top speeds. Best of all, it has helped minimize speed loss over my 10 years of Masters racing, as I close in on the 50-year mark.

How to Swim Taller in Backstroke

Your main trick for swimming taller in backstroke is to have great balance and to increase body roll. So, first make sure your head is hidden and you are leaning on your upper back; this will free up your arms to lengthen your body fully. Then stretch your hand toward the ceiling midway through the recovery, and maintain that reach as your hand enters the water. Finally, as one hand goes in, make sure the shoulder of the other arm rolls clear of the water for recovery. This combination will help increase your body rotation, and optimal rotation in backstroke will also help make you "taller" by a few inches.

The best drill for increasing your awareness of whether or not you're swimming tall in the backstroke is Slide-and-Glide (see page 148). Do it with long pauses — at least two to three counts in your sweet spot before rolling to the other side — and you'll be able to focus on the feeling of being taller and sleeker in your side-balance position. Gradually reduce those pauses bit by bit, moving toward a normal, uninterrupted swimming rhythm while holding fast to that feeling of swimming taller. Count your strokes to see how you're doing. Then add a few 50-yard Swimming Golf repeats (add your time in seconds to your stroke total to get your score) to learn to use that longer vessel to produce more speed.

One of the questions I hear most often about backstroke is whether it pays to practice FQS in this stroke. It might, if it weren't so awkward to do "catch-up" swimming on your back. Backstrokers can, however, benefit from experimenting with a slight overlap in their stroke, and you'll find more info on this in Chapter 12.

Swimming Taller in the Short-Axis Strokes

The most effective way to swim taller in butterfly and breaststroke is to focus on the importance of lengthening your bodyline on each stroke, just as you did in freestyle. In fact, you can make immediate changes just by avoiding one of the most common errors: the tendency to try to create short-axis rotation (*i.e.*, lift the hips) by diving *down* as you initiate the new stroke. Many breaststrokers and flyers see the hip lift that is now common to both strokes and mistakenly think it comes from diving with the hands and shoulders.

It doesn't. Once you learn to produce short-axis rotation by rhythmic body dolphins — particularly *head-lead* body dolphins — you understand that it's downward pressure on the *chest* that creates hip lift. Your hands are simply used to channel that up-and-down motion into linear energy — *i.e.*, moving you down the pool. In both strokes, the fingertips go forward as the chest goes down, and the body follows where the fingertips go. This is precisely the movement pattern that is imprinted onto your neuromuscular system with *Hand-Lead* Body Dolphins. This drill is described on pages 163-165, and is shown on our video *BUTTERFLY AND BREASTSTROKE: the Total Immersion Way.*

How To Swim Taller in Breaststroke

Several stroke techniques in the breaststroke can easily add several inches to the length of your "vessel." First, keep your head as close as possible to a neutral position (the position it's in when you are standing erect) and eliminate "head-nodding" from your stroke. This will help channel your energy *forward, not up and down.*

Second, make sure you stretch your body into a long, clean line for at least a moment during each stroke cycle. Fully extend and streamline both arms as you reach forward; keep stretching until you finish your kick; and squeeze your feet and legs together. The best way to make this position second nature is to practice holding it for at least one or two counts between strokes at moderate speeds.

Third, make sure that your head is directly between your arms, aligned with your spine, and looking directly at the bottom as you reach that stretched-out, glide position. Looking forward during the stretch phase will limit your ability to fully extend.

And, finally, your stroke timing will have a large impact on how "tall" you are in breaststroke. The idea is to "stay as tall as you can for as long as you can" in each stroke cycle, and to minimize time spent in the short position. You are tallest when your bodyline is at full extension. You are shortest when your hands are under your chin and your feet are drawn up toward your buttocks. So the idea is to spend as much of each stroke cycle as possible in the stretched-out position, and as little time as possible in the crunched-up position. And you'll definitely spend too much time in the crunched-up position if you pull too wide or too far back, if your elbows come back alongside your ribs as your hands pass your chin, or if your hands pause after completing the insweep and before shooting forward to the extension.

To teach yourself "swim-taller stroke timing:"
- Keep your pull quick and compact.
- Keep your hands as far in front of you as possible at all times during the pull.

- Keep your hands where you can see them at all times.
- Spin your hands directly to the front as soon as they turn in at the corners (they will sweep in front of your chin first, but the *intent* of sweeping them to the front helps minimize the possibility of pulling too far back).
- Make sure your hands return to full extension before your face is back in the water after each breath.

The quickest, most effective way to become proficient at these skills is to practice them as drills, rather than in whole-stroke swimming. TI's unique drill progression, the same one that has proven so successful at our weekend workshops, team workshops, and summer kids' camps, is described in Chapter 13 and illustrated on the video *BUTTEFLY AND BREASTSTROKE:The Total Immersion Way.*

How To Eliminate Drag in Butterfly

The tendency to dive *down* to make the hips come *up* is most pronounced in butterfly. The best way to overcome that tendency and to maintain a long body is to:

- Think of landing *forward*, not diving down as you re-enter the water.
- Use a wide, flat, sweeping recovery rather than a high, arcing one.
- Practice using a "sneaky breath" (looking down slightly as you breathe) to avoid climbing or lifting as you breathe.
- Keep your shoulders as close as you can to the water's surface at all times.
- Practice Short-Axis Combo swimming; your breaststroke cycles can actually put a bit more length into your fly cycles as well. (Find a detailed description of combo swimming on pages 190-191 and see it illustrated on the video *BUTTERFLY AND BREASTSTROKE: The Total Immersion Way.*)

So far, so good. You've gotten yourself balanced to save energy, letting the water do the work that you once struggled to do. And you've eliminated drag so that the energy saved can be used for speed instead of for making waves. But there are still other ways to become more like a sleek fish and less like a gangly human. Time to begin the last stage of your metamorphosis. Time to get *really* slippery.

Slippery Swimming:
How To Get Faster Without Training Harder

"Reducing the resistance a swimmer must work against is much more effective than increasing the amount of power the swimmer uses to combat that resistance." — TI Coach Emmett Hines

"A swimmer can increase propulsion by increasing force, by reducing drag, or by some combination of the two. Increases of propulsive force can take weeks. Drag can be reduced in a few minutes by orienting the body differently." — Ernie Maglischo, in his book *Swimming Even Faster*

"Swimming velocity may be increased by: 1) increasing the energy put into the water and/or 2) reducing drag. At some point, the swimmer cannot add further energy to the water, because in turbulent water, power transmission becomes increasingly inefficient. A swimmer who reduces drag and turbulence can swim faster on less power than a thrashing, windmilling, inefficient swimmer exerting maximum power." —Ted Isbell, swim coach and engineer

FACT: Even world-class swimmers who swim as efficiently as humanly possible (covering 25 yards of freestyle in as few as seven or eight armstrokes)

use no more than 10 percent of their energy for propulsion. More than 90 percent is consumed by making waves and pushing water aside. And the average lap swimmer, the one taking 25 or more strokes per length? That poor bloke may be squandering as much as 98 percent of his energy output on making waves.

So if you're one of the countless people who would love to swim better but find it difficult, frustrating, or exhausting, it is a virtual certainty that drag is to blame, not your fitness or strength. Drag is the reason why even the world's fastest swimmers can barely manage 5 mph, while some fish hit 50 mph with ease. Fish are so much faster because eons of living under water have shaped them ideally to minimize drag. Arm-thrashing, leg-churning humans are almost as ideally designed to *maximize* drag. And no matter how conscientiously you streamline your body, just the fact that you swim "like a human" still creates a huge amount of water resistance. But there are helpful steps you can take that will make a big difference.

The seeds of those helpful steps were planted in my mind long ago while I was on the seat of a bicycle. I've spent about 40 years enjoying myself on wheels, and for most of that time I've had a general understanding that I could ride more easily, at any speed, when I was tucked over the handlebars than when I was "tall in the saddle." But I didn't fully appreciate how powerfully drag could influence cycling speed until I read that an extraordinarily high percentage of a cyclist's energy output goes into pushing air out of the way. Relatively little actually makes the wheels go around. Ergo, a great deal of cycling speed can be created simply by tucking better to avoid air resistance, instead of laboring to build leg power or aerobic conditioning.

I recall the precise moment when I realized this would be even truer for swimming. In 1978 in Midlothian, Virginia, I began coaching at a pool with an underwater window that was easily accessible from the deck. The first time I went down and watched my team do a set, I was spellbound by a graphic picture that had eluded me all the years I'd coached only from the deck. As I watched my swimmers push off the nearest wall, I could see that the tightly streamlined ones traveled a *looooong* way before they had to begin stroking. And for those brief graceful moments, they actually looked like fish in an aquarium. As soon as they began swimming on the surface, they worked much harder and moved much slower than they had just gliding sleekly under water.

Those who stayed relatively sleek could cover five to eight yards and still look fast and easy. Any swimmers not tightly molded into a torpedo shape

lost speed so dramatically during the pushoff that they looked as if they'd run into a wall. And they had. To a poorly streamlined body, the water *is* a wall. Instantly, I understood that the primary factor determining how fast my swimmers could go was not the training I gave them but the effect of drag on their bodies. I could finally see that the most valuable skill to teach was to streamline — not just on the pushoff, but down the whole length of the pool. It was a logical conclusion, based on the well-known fact that water is about 800 times denser than the "thin" air that costs cyclists such a stunning amount of energy. In a medium as "thick" as water, the payoff for reducing drag at even the slowest speeds can be enormous. And, in a sense, water gets "thicker" as you go faster. Drag increases exponentially as speed goes up, so the good news is that the payoff for *avoiding* drag also increases exponentially the more expertly you avoid it.

Why Water Is a Wall

Boats, cars, and planes all avoid drag best when they are long, sleek, and tapered. Human swimmers can enjoy a moment or two of that as we push off the wall, but as soon as we begin stroking again, most of us revert to blocky and angular shapes. Fast swimmers maintain the most streamlined position as they stroke; slow swimmers do not. And this is the most important distinction between them.

But drag is not just some general retarding force. There are three distinct forms of drag. Two can be minimized by changes in technique, one by changing your suit.

The Three Forms of Drag
1. Form Drag

Form drag is resistance caused by the shape of your non-fishlike body. As you swim, you push water in front of you and pressure builds up. Behind you, your body leaves a turbulent swirl in its wake, creating an area of lower pressure. Higher pressure in front and lower pressure behind creates a vacuum that, in effect, sucks you back. (That's why drafting off other swimmers, as in circle-swimming, makes swimming so much easier. The low-pressure area trailing the swimmer in front of you sucks you *forward*.) Form drag increases as the square of your velocity. Thus, twice as fast means *four* times as much form drag.

Your body's size and shape determine form drag, and the best way to minimize that drag is to slip through the smallest possible "hole" in the water. You do that by staying as close as you can to a balanced, horizontal position, and by making sure all side-to-side movement is beneficial rotation that helps power your stroke —not snaking or fishtailing. Coach Emmett Hines puts it succinctly: "If you're perfectly streamlined — as in the pushoff — *any* motion will increase form drag." That means it's critical, once you begin swimming again after the pushoff, to make your propelling actions as smooth and economical as possible. Concentrate on keeping your shape like a long, sleek racing shell even as you pull and kick, and you'll be on the right track.

Of course the way in which that long, sleek racing shell needs to ride the water differs for long-axis and short-axis strokes. In backstroke and freestyle, you're longest and sleekest when you spend most of each stroke cycle on your side. In breaststroke and butterfly (where swimming on your side obviously isn't an option) slipping just inches under water in a needle-like shape between strokes is the least-drag position.

But be forewarned: To do either one requires impeccable balance for that position.

2. Wave Drag

Just like a boat, you make waves and create a wake while swimming. Wave drag is simply the resistance caused by the waves or turbulence you create. As Hines quips, "Making waves takes energy — *all* of it supplied by you." How much energy depends mainly on how big the waves are: The bigger your wake, the greater your energy loss. Unlike form drag, which increases as the square of velocity, wave drag increases as its *cube*. So as you double your speed, energy spent on wavemaking increases eightfold.

According to Ted Isbell, who coaches TI-style swimming at Channel Islands Aquatics in Ventura, CA, "Wave drag becomes negligible under water, so a swimmer can travel much faster under water than on the surface." That's why the best swimmers in many events now try to stay under water for up to the rules-limited 15 meters after a turn. Under water is also a good place for shorter, more powerful competitors to even things up against the taller, sleeker swimmers who have an advantage on the surface. "Submarines are designed with short, round, fat hulls because they have less surface area than a long, slim vessel," explains Isbell. Good news for shorter and/or stockier swimmers and one of the reasons why such swimmers are often more successful in breaststroke or butterfly (which are swum partially under water), while backstroke and freestyle are often dominated by taller, leaner athletes.

Another key factor in wave drag is how smoothly you stroke. A rough, choppy, or hurried stroke increases turbulence, and turbulent water increases resistance. That's one of the reasons a long stroke is such an advantage: It lets you use a slower, more controlled turnover at any speed, which in turn means less turbulence, fewer waves — and less wave drag.

3. Surface Drag

Surface drag is friction between the water and your skin. No technique can change this law of nature, but you can affect how it applies to you by wearing the right suit. Shed your billowy boxers for a skin-tight racing suit, and just feel the huge difference it makes. Racers, as you probably know, also shave down, and on top of that may don special racing suits made of Teflon-like fabrics to reduce surface drag further still. So slippery is the material when compared to skin, in fact, that an increasing number of elite (and many sub-elite) competitors now wear styles that cover the body from neck to ankles and wrists. For the rest of us, however, a well-fitting lycra suit will do the trick.

Tuning in to Drag

Besides the drag-defeating strategies noted above, the simplest and best strategy for slipping more easily through that wall of water is to pay strict attention to every lap you swim. Alexander Popov may be the world's fastest swimmer, but he often practices swimming "super slowly" at speeds where he can feel the resistance trying to hold him back, so he can figure out what he can do to minimize it. Even without Popov's super-sensitive "drag antennae" to pick up signals, however, there are ways you can heighten your own sensitivity to drag.

First, intentionally create more drag. Push off the wall with your arms wide and head high. Wow! That's *drag*! Then push off in the most stream-lined position, and compare the resistance. Use that "awareness training" in your regular swimming to cue in to the ways in which the water resists you, and to the stroke changes — such as keeping your head in a neutral position or using your hands to "part the waters" before stroking — that enable you to feel less of it.

To experience drag, try pushing off with arms wide and head high.

Push off in streamlined position and compare the resistance.

Second, use your ears. That's right. How much noise do you make while swimming? Do you splash, plop, and plunk? Sound is energy, and the less of your mechanical energy you convert into noise, the more remains to move you forward. More to the point, anything that results in noisy swimming is evidence of inefficiency. Working on "silent swimming" is one of the best ways to tune in more acutely to how you're flowing through the water, and can help you improve your fluency.

Splash equals energy loss when you swim.

Third, use your eyes. Are there bubbles in your stroke? Goggles make it easy to tell, and marathon swimmer and TI coach Don Walsh uses his to observe one of the most available pieces of "swimming knowledge" you can have about yourself. In fact, for a full year of practice, Don focused more on eliminating bubbles from his stroke than almost anything else, which is probably why he was able to complete the 28.5-mile Manhattan Island Marathon in *14,000* fewer strokes than his rivals.

That number is no figment. Walsh actually calculated it, by having his boat crew monitor his stroke rate and compare it with that of the other swimmers. He swam just as fast at 50 strokes per minute as other swimmers did at about 72 strokes per minute. That means in the nine hours it took Walsh to swim up the East River and down the Hudson, he took something on the order of 27,000 strokes, while virtually every other swimmer in the race — including many who finished behind him! — ended up needing about 41,000. That many strokes would have sent Don halfway around Manhattan again! Viewed another way, he got a "free ride" of almost 10 miles by being so slippery. If, like Don, you can learn to slip through the water rather than battling it, you'll see far fewer bubbles through your goggles, and there will be much less turbulence in your wake.

Bubbles indicate too much effort and inefficiency.

No bubbles indicate balance and ease.

Finally, imagine your body has a kind of shadow trailing behind you as you swim. Remember: you're creating a wake similar to that of a boat, and though it spreads a bit as it reaches your feet, it doesn't spread much. Consider that wake your shadow, and anything that slips outside of it as drag. Your feet, for instance, may be moving you along as you kick, but as soon as they slip outside your "shadow", they increase drag.

As soon as your kick slips outside your "shadow," it becomes drag.

The Choice Is Yours

As coaches Hines, Maglischo, and Isbell noted at the beginning of this chapter, swimmers have a choice to make each time they arrive at the pool: You can spend your time training hard and long to muscle up your propulsive force and inflate your aerobic capacity, or you can spend your time reducing the sheer physical effort it takes to swim, while increasing your focus on trimming drag and reducing the energy spent on wavemaking.

A single trip to any aquarium – or to the underwater window of any lap pool — will provide dramatic proof that the smarter path by far is the path of least resistance.

Up to this point you've been focusing on good "vessel design," exploring all the ways of keeping yourself balanced, long, and sleek. Now that your "hull" is as efficient as it can be, it's time to put the engine in and find out how to run it with the same, smart efficiency.

DRAG AS A TRAINING TOOL?

Training that increases drag on swimmers has always been in vogue to some degree. One of the most common ploys is having swimmers wear clothes – sometimes T-shirts and shoes, sometimes pantyhose, but more often "drag suits" resembling today's billowy basketball shorts. A surprising number of adult swimmers come to TI workshops in long, voluminous trunks, possibly thinking it's good training, possibly thinking they're not "good enough" or "serious enough" to merit a racing brief.

The practice seems to be spreading. More and more coaches are intentionally having their swimmers wear drag shorts in practice, primarily to make them work harder. (Harder is supposedly always better, remember?) More drag should develop more strength, the thinking goes, and when the suit comes off, *voila*! More speed. Plus, the sensation of "feeling" faster racing in a brief as opposed to spinnaker-like pantaloons is expected to give a psychological lift. But suppose bad habits, developed while wearing the "drag suit," cause whatever strength the suit helps you gain to be used ineffectively? Not much advantage there, right? Well, truth to tell, that's just what happens in most cases.

"Drag training" has seldom been examined critically. The reality the coaches who use it may be missing is that, as I have just explained, every swimmer – even shaved-down swimmers in space-age bodysuits — already experiences *plenty* of drag. And it's the instinctive efforts of these swimmers to overcome that drag that damage their fluency and efficiency, making them "practice struggle" in various ways. Not what anyone intends, obviously, but in the vast majority of cases, that's exactly what happens. And because drag can square (or even cube!) as velocity increases, the resistance the water throws at you will always be ahead of the strength you've built to overcome it. Efforts to increase power will always help less than efforts to reduce drag.

It takes a special *kind* of strength, skillfully applied, to overcome the water's resistance. So even swimmers who have already made great strides in drag reduction need to approach power-oriented training with care. Does the artificial drag develop muscles that help produce a long, smooth, efficient stroke? Or, like drag suits and most other clothes, does the equipment not only hold you back but also weigh you down, so you end up strengthening the muscles you use struggling to stay horizontal and not sink? That's a perfect way to do your stroke more harm than good. Remember, for an unskilled swimmer — which includes most folks who come to TI workshops wearing

Chapter 6

Engaging the Kinetic Chain:
How To Turn on Effortless Power

S
o far, our strategy for mastering smooth and fast "fishlike swim-ming" has focused on ways to make your body more slippery by minimizing the resistance water throws in its way. At TI, we always teach these so-called "eliminating" skills first because common sense, and our coaching experience, have shown us convincingly that this is how swim-mers improve most. Right from our first workshop in 1989, we noticed that when we help swimmers become more slippery, we also see a dramatic im-provement in their stroke length. When we teach them to propel better, the gain is far more modest. Yet as we've said, the average swimmer seldom thinks about slipperiness and its flip side, drag, and most coaches and teachers hardly mention it. So the biggest potential improvement breakthrough just gets ignored.

But once you've eliminated all the drag you can, it's time to turn onto the more familiar path of improvement: how you propel yourself through the water and, more important, how to tap an effortless power source as you do.

That's not to imply, however, that eliminating drag and increasing pro-pulsion are unrelated. They're not. If you were truly a "vessel" we could dis-cuss them separately because, with a boat, what minimizes drag — the shape of the hull — never changes. And whether the propulsion is an engine and a propeller, sails, or oars, the hull shape stays the same.

But you're not a sloop or a rowing shell, you're a swimmer, and for better

baggy shorts — absolutely nothing is more important than learning basi
ance. Loose suits that drag down the hips just make that tougher. My ad
Stick with a racing brief.

But let's say you've finally crossed the threshold. You're now one of th
practiced, enviably efficient swimmers who are discriminating enough to
helped and not harmed by training with increased drag. What can you d
Three things:

1. **Just swim faster.** Since drag increases with velocity, the simplest way to
add drag is to add velocity — swim faster. Any under-distance repeat that
allows you to swim faster than your race pace will do. For distance races
(800 meters and up), brisk, strong, 100-yard/meter repeats will work. For
a middle-distance swimmer (200 to 500 yards), 25- or 50-yard repeats,
swum faster than race pace, are the ticket. And sprinters (50 or 100 yards/
meters) can do ultra-short repeats — perhaps as few as three to five stroke
cycles — at top speed. But always keep strokes as long and smooth as
possible, even though you're taking them at a higher stroke rate. If you
discipline yourself to do these shorter repeats at two or three fewer
strokes/length, than you take while racing, you'll be using the $V = SL \times SR$
equation to great advantage, practicing superior Stroke Length, combined
with a Stroke Rate high enough to move you faster than race speed. That
will produce some really valuable muscle memory.

2. **Use paddles or fins.** They increase the area of your propelling surfaces
so your hand or foot meets more resistance as it moves through the water. Plus, they help you move faster, and more speed, remember, means
more drag. Again, shorter repeats will help you gain the greatest benefit
because you can swim at higher speed, for a shorter time, and minimize
form breakdowns. The key, once again, is to count your strokes. Keep
the count much lower (perhaps 20% to 30%) than when you're swimming without fins or paddles to ensure that the muscles you build are
"long stroke" ones.

3. **Try a swim tether.** Anchoring yourself to one wall with latex tubing,
then swimming away against the growing resistance of the tube, may be
the purest way to subject your stroke to muscle-building drag. Simple
guidelines: Count your strokes, and keep your form smooth no matter
how tough it gets to move forward. And the payoff — being pulled back
down the pool at high speed by the recoiling tether — is not only a fun
ride, but instructive as well. It can glaringly reveal which areas of your
body are guilty of the most resistance.

or worse you cannot separate the act of propelling from the act of eliminating. The stroking and kicking movements that move you through the water also constantly change your shape, and that means form drag is constantly changing, too. Wave drag can also vary significantly, depending on how rough or smooth, how hurried or controlled, your propelling actions are.

Actually, it's a good thing that "eliminating" and "propelling" skills aren't separate and distinct, because you don't have to do two separate and distinct types of training. You will learn the "propelling" skills of being more fishlike by focusing on many of the very same skill objectives you used to "eliminate," but you will think about them differently. Though most of your concentration will still go toward the skills of staying slippery, simply because those skills are less intuitive, they will gradually grow into habits. And as they do you'll be able to concentrate more on making your propelling actions smooth, controlled, and fluent. Most of all, you'll learn to instinctively use the most effortless and powerful motor you have: your core body.

Want a quick and exciting preview of how to do that? Visit an aquarium. Watching fish from under water leaves one powerful impression: The best "engine" for propulsion in a fluid is the core body. Lacking arms and legs, fish cannot propel themselves by pulling and kicking as humans do; they use rhythmic body undulation to move. And as we all know, they move with stunning speed and hypnotic grace and ease.

Watch the world's best swimmers from poolside at an elite-level meet and you'll see much the same thing. Their strokes are a virtual symphony: the torso sets the rhythm, the arms and legs move in harmony. Then drop in at the local Y to watch average swimmers during lap-swim time, and you'll see just the opposite: arms flailing, legs churning, and the core bodies in between uselessly locked in place.

So, let's get to work on a whole-body tune-up of the power train — engine to propeller.

The Kinetic Chain: Your True Source of Swimming Power

It's only natural to think of our arms and legs as the "engine" for fast swimming. And virtually all of us instinctively move our arms and legs faster when we want to go faster. The countless yards that swimmers devote to pulling with a foam buoy immobilizing their legs, or kicking with arms holding a board, are powerful evidence of our ingrained belief that it's important to work, really *work*, on strengthening our pull or our kick. And the concept is ingrained not just in our minds, but also in our nervous systems and muscle memory. For that reason, the shift from arm-dominated to core-based propulsion will take time, patience, persistence, and attention. But I promise you that the rewards will be more than worth it.

If you *really* want to learn to swim more like a fish, consider again how fish actually swim. They scoot through the water in the most uncomplicated way imaginable, simply by rhythmically oscillating or undulating their entire body. That produces tail-whip, and off they go. Fishlike propulsion for humans is based on the same principle: core-body rotation for long-axis strokes, undulation for short-axis strokes.

In an ideal world it wouldn't be necessary for a swimmer to *learn* hip rotation. Rolling from side to side is, after all, the most natural way for your body to accommodate the alternating-arm actions of freestyle and backstroke. Prove this to yourself by standing in place and moving your arms as if swimming freestyle. Swivel your hips and you'll move your arms far more freely; keep the hips immobile and you'll feel restricted. Because rolling is a natural tendency, a freestyler must actually expend energy to remain flat (usually by splaying their arms or legs). In most cases this is not intentional or even conscious; "flat" swimmers remain flat because they haven't mastered side-lying balance. As soon as they become comfortable with side-lying balance, something that is not natural or instinctive in most people but that can be learned, they stop fighting themselves and roll more freely.

Though coaches speak of hip rotation as a way to swim more powerfully, in truth it has an even greater advantage: Your body slips through the water more easily in the side-lying position. And remember: Techniques that reduce drag are always more beneficial to speed than those that increase power.

But that doesn't mean you turn down more power when it's handed to you on a plate, and that's just what hip roll does. For once you have become more slippery by gaining the freedom to take advantage of your body's natural roll, you also gain access to an incredibly powerful "engine" for swimming propulsion — the kinetic chain. That's just a technical way of saying that the power we use in, say, our pitching arm actually originates as far away as our feet. It gradually gets magnified as it travels up the chain for delivery, ultimately allowing us to uncork a blistering fastball.

The world's best swimmers have an instinctive awareness of the power of the kinetic chain and how to use it. While we typically muscle our way along, using our arms and shoulders to do most of the work of swimming, super-efficient swimmers get their power in the torso and use their arms and shoulders to transmit this force to the water. Great technique can be a great equalizer. Mastery of the kinetic chain is what allows Tiger Woods, for example, to drive a golf ball farther than rivals who are far bigger and stronger.

The kinetic chain is not a complicated concept. In fact, you and I both learned to use it, probably as preschoolers, the first time we figured out how to propel ourselves on a playground swing. I can't recall the learning process precisely, but it probably started with vigorous leg kicking, which just made the swing shake a bit, but certainly not soar. But I can vividly recall how satisfying it was when I got it right and experienced, for the first time, the effect of engaging *every* muscle in finely timed, coordinated action. This happened when I figured out that if I leaned forward slightly, that made the swing move back a little. As gravity pulled it down again, I helped it along by leaning back. Each time gravity reversed us, we added enough leverage to make it go a little farther. And farther. And farther. The most satisfying moments of all? I don't know about you, but I remember them well. It was when I reached the apogee of the backward swings, having figured out how to put *all* my muscle and mass into a perfectly linked series of arcs. The simple desire to go higher and faster taught me to pull on the chain with my hands and tighten my stomach muscles to link the tension of my backward-pulling arms all the way to the stretching toes of my forward-straining legs, and time it all to add my power to the accelerating force of gravity. The skill, simple enough to be learned by any child, produced a breathtakingly fast and powerful swoop through space, with such marvelous efficiency that I could continue endlessly without tiring. The kinetic chain, I had found, is a remarkable force. Just imagine what it can do for your swimming when you learn to use it fully.

Effortless power for fishlike swimming is produced in much the same way. Energy for the most powerful movements doesn't start and stop in any one joint, but ripples through our bodies like a cracked whip until it finally arrives at the point where it's released. In freestyle and backstroke, body rotation provides a big chunk of the power — as it does when we throw a rock, a javelin, or a karate blow. In all these cases, the legs and hips power the torso, which drives the arm. In the body undulation of butterfly and breaststroke, the arms are powered simultaneously by a "force coupler" in which core muscles link hips and shoulders in the same way as when you're doing a pull-up, double-poling on skis...or soaring on a playground swing.

Chapter 7

Developing an Effective Pull:
It's All About Holding Patterns,
Not "S" Patterns

If Power Comes From the Core,
What Comes From the Arms?

Because swimmers sense that their biggest job in the water is using their hands to push water back, they give that motion most of their attention. Working on "technique" therefore means tweaking the armstroke, and "power" means putting more muscle, force, and acceleration into the motion — the better to push your body forward. Between what instinct suggests, and instruction tells you, the arms and hands do seem to be 90% of swimming. So let's examine how the arms and hands can be used more effectively, making optimal use of the power generated by the kinetic chain.

The first thing to do is to ignore most of the advice found in the kinds of swimming books (weighty texts by all the authoritative sources) that fill the shelf above the desk where I write. True, they offer thousands of pages of minutely detailed information about swimming technique, and all share a keen fascination with what the hands do: angle of attack, sweeps, pitches, vectors and vortices, lift forces, etc. But that's just the trouble. The hands of extraordinarily gifted swimmers unquestionably *do* move in highly efficient and intricate paths, which researchers film and analyze in staggering detail and breathlessly report on in papers, articles, and books. But as any practical coach knows, the only sensible reaction to all that minutiae is, "So what?"

How can I say that? Well, take the debate that heated up in the mid 1990s over the role of the hands in propulsion. One of the central doctrines handed down by researchers for the previous 20 years, that swimming propulsion results primarily from lift forces (hand-sculling actions) rather than drag forces (pushing-back actions), was suddenly challenged by dissenting scholars. Point and counterpoint studies and papers filled hundreds of pages in journals. Besieged coaches understandably began to conclude, *"This stuff must be really important!"*

Why would it be important, I found myself almost alone in asking? It seemed obvious to me then, as it does now, that this welter of detail might be academically interesting, but realistically useless. I don't care if it's lift- *or* drag-propelled, the action they're talking about happens so quickly that no swimmer could possibly control the fine adjustments needed to transform one to the other. And the most accomplished swimmers don't really give this stuff a second thought anyway. Their wonderful technique comes not from dogma cited in a study, but from intuition and perception. In the end, they just do what *feels* best.

Case in point: While preparing an article on backstroke technique in July 1999, I interviewed Lenny Krayzelburg just weeks before he set world records in both the 100-meter and 200-meter backstroke. As we talked about what he liked to feel while swimming, he related that one of the leading coach/scientists had been urging him to adopt an "exciting new technique" that involved adding an extra scull at the finish of his stroke to enhance its "lift." So Lenny practiced it diligently for weeks. And you know what? Research or no, he summarily decided to give it up. All the science in the world couldn't overcome the fact that "It felt all wrong." What looks good in theory or in the lab often feels distracting to the swimmer in the water.

Besides, even if swimmers did have the concentration and precise muscular control to make the fine adjustments needed to use more lift (or drag), it would barely make a difference. No matter how assiduously you may tweak your hand movements, at the end of the day it's still just a little hand pushing against *water*...trying to propel a big body through a resistant medium.

Learn to "Anchor" Your Hands

My mentor Bill Boomer said, "The hips are your engine; your hands are just the propeller. Always keep your hands connected to their power source." And one of the surest ways to disconnect your propeller from your engine is overly aggressive arm-stroking. A "controlled" stroke, one that stays connected to its power source through its full length, is one that begins with an "anchored" hand.

That power-producing kinetic chain, you see, must always start from a fixed (or "anchored") point. When you're on land, that anchor point is usually your feet, planted on the ground. The initiating action twists the body away from the intended direction of the movement. With the feet fixed in place, you get an effect known as elastic loading, similar to storing energy in a rubber band by stretching it. The cocked hip then acts like a whip handle, throwing energy upward through torso, shoulders, and arms, with increasing speed and power.

Swimmers, of course, have no foot-to-ground anchor, so the hips cannot act as a whip handle. But though the hips can't magnify power, they can deliver the power they already have by moving as a unit with the entire torso. Still, the process must start with an anchoring point to enable that fingers-to-toes band of engaged muscle we used to such dynamic effect on the playground swing. In fishlike swimming that power linkage starts with an "anchored hand." While your instincts tell you to grab water and push it back *hard*, you can actually tap far more effortless power by reaching your hands to their full extension, and then just *holding on* to your place in the water. Rather than immediately pushing back, try to make your hands stand still as if grasping a ladder rung. Then let the kinetic chain kick in to roll you past the spot where your hands are anchored.

This isn't some kind of New Age theory. It's fact. In 1970, famed Indiana University swim coach Doc Counsilman filmed with an underwater camera swimming legend Mark Spitz, the world's greatest swimmer at the time. Attaching tiny lights to Spitz's hands to highlight their movements, Counsilman shot him from the side against a grid-like backdrop. When he developed the film, Counsilman was startled to see that Spitz's hands apparently exited the water *forward* of where they had entered. Spitz could not possibly be pushing his hands back, if they came out ahead of their entry point.

Nor could Joao Gloria, a 10-year-old from Portugal who attended one of our TI kids' camps and who quickly developed one of the most fishlike strokes we've ever seen. Despite his youth and small size, he was easily able to swim 25 yards of freestyle in 11 strokes. How could he possibly do this? Watching from the side on underwater video, it was easy to see that his hands entered and exited at the same place, while has body slid sleekly past their anchoring point on each stroke.

Accomplished short-axis swimmers can achieve exactly the same thing. Watching world-champion breaststroker Kristi Kowal on underwater video I took at a National Team training camp, I saw her stretch her hands far forward, sweep them outside her shoulders to her "catch," then use her abdominal muscles to bring her hips forward to where her hands were anchored, very much as if she were doing a stomach crunch. Even as her hands swept inward toward her chin, they stayed abreast of the same lane marker where they began the stroke.

Develop "Feel" of the Water

Easy to describe, but perhaps not so easy to learn? Training yourself to make your hand stand still rather than pushing it back does seem a very odd notion. How can your body go in one direction unless your hand goes in the other?

No, the water is not a ladder. And no, you're not pulling yourself along it, rung by rung. But when you develop an acute "feel of the water," you *can* actually swim like that. Instead of slipping past you, your hand is "fastened" in place, and you can use your grip on the water to move yourself very nearly as a rock climber uses his hold on the rock.

But that seems to be a well-kept secret. Coaches, after all, tend to describe "feel of the water" as a prize with a staggering price. They can't define it *exactly*, but they seem to suggest you must either have been born with a mystical gift for controlling elusive water molecules, like herding fireflies, or must spend millions of yards somehow acquiring this special knack.

There is no doubt that most elite swimmers have a variety of gifts that help them perform on a higher plane, and "feel of the water" is probably the most important of them all. But it's not a hard gift to explain. It is, simply, a heightened kinesthetic awareness, an ability to sense minute differences in water pressure, and to seek more of that pressure with the body's propelling surfaces and less of it with the rest of the body. Maximum power, minimum drag.

There is also no doubt that any motivated and attentive student can learn to greatly increase his or her own feel for the best way to work *with* the water. Feel of the water, in other words, can be an acquired skill. And it needn't take years to acquire. Here are the key ways you can get a better grip on the ability to hold the water:

1. **Get the catch right.** Swimmers usually give about 90 percent of their technique attention to the armstroke, and by now you know I think that's a waste of time. Instead, I recommend you pay far more attention to drag

because that brings faster, better results. But, when you *do* devote some time to learning to propel more effectively (for the most part after you are balanced, tall, slippery, and moving with some degree of fluency) give 90% of *that* attention to the moment when you make the "catch." Focus on your hands while they're in front of your head (you'll find guidance below on what to focus on), and once they've passed your shoulders, just let them fall off your mental radar screen. Once properly initiated, a stroke doesn't really need much further guidance.

2. **Start each stroke by making your hands stand still.** Your instincts tell you to grab the water and push back. Ignore your instincts. Teach yourself instead to make your hands stay right where they entered the water. Bring your body over them. Try to begin each stroke as if there was a rung or something else solid to hold on to. But more than anything, resist the urge to muscle the water back.

3. **Drill, drill, drill.** Learning a skill as elusive and refined as this one takes a *lot* of concentration and focus. You get the most intensive focus in drills, where you repeat simple movements with full attention instead of trying to "read" something that happens in a millisecond while swimming whole stroke. For the long-axis strokes, the Easy Anchors drills (see pages 126 and 146) are the simplest way to train yourself to connect your hands to your core body, and move them in perfect coordination. For freestyle, the Switch drills (see pages 130-144) then give you a dynamic way to learn to anchor your hands and bring your body over them. For backstroke, the drills Slide and Glide (page 148) and Single-Arm Backstroke (see page 151) allow you to put great focus on the moment when your hands "trap and wrap" the water. For both short-axis strokes, the Find Your Corners drill (page 166) is specifically designed to teach the anchoring skill that links the hands to the hips. To multiply the effect of any drills — particularly drills used to teach anchoring — do them with fistgloves (see box on pages 67-68).

4. **Swim super slowly.** Drills will teach you how things feel when they're "right." When you then begin to apply what you've learned in drills, you'll hold on to far more of what you need to feel if you swim *verrry* slowly. The more slowly you swim, the more "concentration space" you give yourself to cultivate a finer sense of water pressure on the catch. Just be very patient. Leave your hand out in front of you. S-t-r-e-t-c-h that moment, pressing gently on the water until you feel the water return some of that

pressure to your hands. And while you're swimming slowly...

5. **Count your strokes**. A very low stroke count is one of the simpler and more reliable indicators that you're *not* pulling back. If you've whittled your count in a 25-yard pool down to, say, 12 or fewer strokes in freestyle, one of the things you're likely to be doing well is holding on to the water. As you go faster (and your stroke count increases) stay hyper-alert to any sense of water slippage on your hands. That's like a car spinning its wheels, and just as undesirable.

6. **Try to have slow hands.** Compare the speed at which you sense your hands moving back, with how fast your body is moving forward. Try to have "slow hands and a faster body" or at the very least match the speed of your hands to the speed of your body. This is a great corrective any time you feel your stroke getting too rough and ragged.

"Anchoring" Tools: Should it Be Fistgloves or Paddles?

No suspense about this one: fistgloves are unquestionably the way to *quickly* learn how to anchor your hands. They turn any swimmer into a problem solver, and when the problem the fistgloves create is solved, the ungloved hand will be much more solidly anchored.

One of my favorite coaching techniques is to present swimmers with a well-designed challenge, *e.g.*, figuring out how to make forward progress in the water without the use of an open hand. It never fails...swimmers will experiment with different solutions and intuitively discover the one that works best (and it won't necessarily be the same solution for every swimmer). Then, through practice, they'll come to "own" the improved technique that results, and they'll remember the lesson because they discovered the answer all by themselves. In my experience, self-discovered technique is invariably more natural to the swimmer than one imposed by a coach or teacher.

The problem presented to the swimmer by the fistglove® stroke trainer is: How do you hold on to the water when you have nothing to hold on with? By squeezing the hands into a tight, latex-wrapped fist, fistgloves turn a broad, flat surface into a rubber nub. On the first few lengths, your hands slip helplessly through the water. But, gradually, you figure out how to gain a little control, partly by using the forearm for purchase, partly by increasing the rotation of your body, and partly by simply learning to be more patient. By making the catch with exquisite patience and attention, you will eventually learn to get the water to resist the gloved hand *just a little bit*. With practice you can learn to do remarkable things with the slight amount of resistance. So much so that by continuing to stroke patiently, the gloved-swimming sensation will gradually come to feel almost "normal." After a while, you may even wonder if you're wearing a glove. Measure how much control you're gaining by counting strokes per length. If your experience is similar to my own and that of my TI swimming colleagues, you'll find that when you first start wearing fistgloves, your stroke count per 25 yards may be 3 to 4 strokes higher than without the gloves. But, after regular and attentive practice with the gloves, our gloved count is now only 1 or 2 or 0 counts higher than our ungloved count. We've learned to balance and rotate and find the best path through the water with our arms.

The real magic, of course, happens when you peel off the gloves. Suddenly, the previously ordinary-feeling hand seems *huge*, as if you had a dinner-plate-sized paddle at the end of your arm. And with that broad, flat, blade-like implement to work with, holding on to the water — anchoring your hand — turns out to be a piece of cake.

Why are fistgloves better than paddles for teaching feel of the water? Because paddles teach the opposite lesson from fistgloves. Swimmers figure that paddles will teach them how it feels to have "big hands," and that once the paddles come off they'll remember the sensation they're aiming for. While the paddles are on, you do of course feel much more able to hold the water. But when the paddles come off? You feel like someone rowing with a popsicle stick. Your hands seem dumb, ineffectual. We have taken to calling fistgloves the "unpaddles," because after using fistgloves your hands seem smarter, not dumber.

Chapter 8

Developing an Effective Kick:
Less Is Usually More

M ost swimmers, down deep, really do suspect their legs don't help them out much in the speed department. But because the kick obviously pushes them forward to some degree, they don't dare gamble on not doing kicking sets. Besides, the fastest swimmers in any group or on any team usually also seem to be the fastest when the kickboards are handed out. So they must know something, right?

In fact, your kick does contribute something to propulsion, but not in the way most of us imagine. My sense is that most people vaguely think they need a good kick because either:

1. If my arms can propel my body at 4 feet per second and my legs can propel it at 2 feet per second, maybe together they can propel it at 6 feet per second.

2. If I really work hard at those kickboard training sets, I'll get a more powerful "outboard motor," say a 40-horsepower Evinrude instead of the 20-hp model I have when I don't train hard with a kickboard.

But it doesn't pan out quite that way. Yes, a swimmer kicking on a board creates propulsion, sometimes even really fast propulsion. The best kickers in the world can go one minute or faster for 100 yards on a kickboard, faster than most of us can swim. But that tells us nothing about how much a stronger kick *adds* to whole-stroke swimming, nor the energy cost of whatever good it does do.

More than 50 years ago Doc Counsilman, the legendary Indiana University swim coach, designed an experiment to actually measure what kicking adds to propulsion. He devised an apparatus to tow swimmers in a glide position at various speeds, both with kicking and without kicking. Tension on the line was measured to see if it was greater, less, or the same when kicking as it was when just gliding along.

The only instance in which kicking decreased tension on the line (*i.e.*, added propulsion) was at slow towing speeds, with the swimmer kicking at maximum effort. But at any speed over 5 feet per second (1:00 per 100 yards) the kick contributed nothing and, in some instances, actually *increased* drag!

Counsilman interpreted these results using an automotive metaphor. Imagine, he suggested, a car with separate front- and rear-wheel drive. If the front wheels turn at 30 mph, but the rear wheels turn at 20 mph, the car's total speed will be not 50 but less than 30 mph, because the rear wheels create drag. The same thing happens, he contended, when a swimmer with a reasonably fast upper body persists in emphasizing a less-efficient kick. The kick consumes energy and creates drag. More work, less speed.

How much energy the kick costs has also been measured. Several different studies over the past 30 years have gauged the oxygen consumption of competitive swimmers while pulling only, kicking only, and swimming whole stroke. Each study found that hard kicking greatly increases the energy cost of moving at a given speed. In one study, kicking at a speed of about 60 seconds for 50 yards — a rather moderate speed for any competitive swimmer — used four times as much oxygen as pulling at the same speed.

The obvious conclusion: Kicking can add only a modest amount of propulsion to an efficient stroke, while it can add a significant amount of drag and enormously increase the energy cost of whole-stroke swimming, if over-emphasized. Therefore swimmers should do all they can to maximize the benefit of their kicking while minimizing the work they put into it.

Kick for Efficiency, Not for Speed

"Fine," you say. "If all kicking does is burn energy and cause drag, why bother to kick at all?" Well, because that's *not* all kicking does. An efficient kick will improve your stroke and, in fact, is essential for the kinetic chain to produce anything like the power it's capable of producing for you.

To understand this, you have only to imagine a baseball pitcher trying to throw a fastball with his legs shackled. Or Venus Williams trying to hit a tennis serve without being allowed to step into it. Or you, trying to swoop and soar on a playground swing while holding your legs tucked tightly under you.

The key is to allow your legs to move in the most natural, efficient way while avoiding non-essential movement. An efficient, impeccably timed kick can make the action of the kinetic chain far more potent, and cost very little energy. Skeptical? Stand with your feet a bit more than hip-width apart and let your arms hang loosely, with room to swing them freely. Keeping your feet flat on the floor, rotate your body right and left, letting your arms swing out freely as you do. You'll feel the relatively rigid, fixed position of your legs impeding your movement, creating tension from your knees to your hips.

Now repeat the movement, but allow your back heel to lift as you swing. You'll find that you rotate freely at least an additional 30 degrees in each direction, and eliminate the inhibiting tension.   Repeat the experiment one last time, but now add just a little *push* off the ball of the rear foot whenever it feels most natural to do so. When you time this gentle push correctly to the body swing, you'll feel yourself rotate with even more speed and power.

Just for fun before you quit, try the same rotation/swing while fluttering your feet rapidly in place. See what happens? Right. Your coordination and efficiency break down and the movement degenerates into a sloppy, shapeless mess. Uncoordinated leg movements always scuttle the rhythmic, driving momentum you can create when your legs and torso move with great coordination.

And that shows precisely what can happen when an efficient kick coordinates well with great body rotation – in both long-axis and short-axis strokes. It also shows what can happen with an inefficient kick — no matter how well conditioned it may have become through miles of diligent kickboard training. The inefficient kick will be very good at adding drag and energy cost and contributing nothing to propulsion or speed. And it will be very good as well at making you much more tired, much more quickly. I know from years c observation that the final, uncoordinated twitching I suggested you try ab° is exactly what happens to an unbalanced swimmer. An unbalanced swir° will sense his or her legs are sinking, and react by moving them eve° frantically. The uncoordinated kick that results not only fails to cor° balance, but also destroys any possibility of smooth, fluid body ro° it needn't happen at all to a swimmer who has truly mastered h° balanced swimmer's legs are freed of *having* to kick this way freely. When they do, they can find the movement pattern ' best with body movement.

The first example above — swinging with feet flat and fixed — is equivalent to a swimmer trying *not* to kick (or perhaps wearing a pull buoy). Legs held rigidly in place will add tension or torque that impedes the free rotation of the body, and muscle tension is nothing more than work with no benefit. The free-heel movement is the equivalent of a natural, *non-overt,* 2-beat kick, moving in coordination with body roll. This kind of kick feels effortless, almost unconscious, and is the best for most people when swimming longer distances or when doing fitness or lap swimming. The third example, adding a well-timed *push* to your body swing, is the equivalent of putting a bit more snap into the downbeat of your 2-beat kick. If you add it at just the right time and put in just the right additional amount of effort, you'll feel your hips drive with more power. And if you keep your armstroke connected to body roll as you're supposed to, increased hip drive will translate, finally, into a more powerful stroke.

But it's critical that you first establish impeccable timing in your 2-beat kick, and that you can sense where to add the extra snap just as easily as you can while standing in the middle of the room and swinging back and forth.

Long-Axis Kicking

So, how do you develop a good kick? Nearly 30 years of coaching have convinced me that a swimmer's kick is not nearly so susceptible to "molding" or skill-improvement as other parts of the stroke. In almost every case, the kicking ability or tendencies I've seen a swimmer display in his or her first year of training have been little changed 5 or 10 years later. Coaching has often helped smooth out the rough spots and minimize correctable inefficiencies, but it virtually never resulted in a swimmer with a middling kick somehow learning a great one. A great kick seems to be one of those things with which you are either born or you are not.

So, as a coach, I have mainly tried to help swimmers find their own best ~~v~~ to kick, and then to coordinate that kick as smoothly as possible with the ~~a~~ll stroke. *Kick*board training, particularly in the long-axis strokes, has ~~b~~een an effective aid to that process. The flutter kick that you practice ~~k~~board is so different from the kind you use when you swim freestyle ~~s~~ke that kickboard sets have next to no value for developing an ~~~~ (*i.e.,* one that properly assists the kinetic chain, with the lowest ~~~~d without increasing drag).

~~~~ say, "if the kickboard doesn't teach me to kick, what does?" ~~~~bably able to anticipate my answer: drills. The kind of kick-

ing you practice in drills uses your legs to help in practicing balance, rotation, and much more dynamic movement than is possible on a kickboard. And if you're concerned about conditioning, don't be. The kicking you do while swimming at moderate, sustainable speeds readies your legs to do that same kind of kicking in longer races. And when you're pouring on the speed, you're conditioning your legs for the demands that sprint races will place on your legs. At West Point, we never did a single kickboard set. Yet none of my swimmers ever complained that his or her legs "died" in a race. They simply trained, with fluent swimming at a variety of speeds, to use their bodies as efficiently integrated units. Their legs provided just the help that was needed at each speed and, as they did, became conditioned for the work each kind of swimming required.

So if you're not to worry about conditioning, what about execution? Is there one particular kicking style in the long-axis strokes that's kind of a gold standard? No, there isn't. For although freestyle and backstroke use virtually the same kick, virtually all backstrokers favor the steady, unbroken 6-beat kick, while among competitive freestylers, the number using either 6-beat or 2-beat kicks is fairly even. Among fitness and lap swimmers, the 2-beat is much more common than the 6-beat. Different strokes, as they say, for different folks.

When it comes to the top freestyle sprinters, you'll find a strong 6-beat kick almost universal. But there's more at work here than the beat. The best sprinters in the world (who, you'll remember, also tend to be among the tallest swimmers) almost always have large, supple feet, great ankle flexibility, and consequently a great kick. A superb flutter kick, in fact, seems to be one of the great assets of highly accomplished sprinters.

My sense is that a great kick like this is less important for the propulsion it may contribute, than for its effect in raising more of the sprinter's body out of the water. Because drag builds exponentially with increases in speed, the sprinter encounters far more drag than the slower distance swimmer. So one of the things sprinters must do to achieve those speeds is reduce drag by lifting as much of the body as possible above the surface. And since the hydroplaning effect requires many times more velocity than the human-swimming limit of 5 mph, a swimmer can't depend on lift created by forward motion. So, we create some lift with a powerful kick. The energy cost for doing so is enormous, but the race will be over in less than a minute anyway so it's an affordable cost.

The primary danger among sprinters, by the way, is emphasizing the kick too much, which increases drag and energy cost and decreases coordination and control. A too-powerful kick is just as bad as too slight a kick when sprinting, and in both cases the remedy is the same: to make whatever kick you have fit in as seamlessly as possible with the overall stroke. Whenever I see someone swimming with a kick that's too visible, too apparent, it shouts "wasted energy" to me. So I tell them, "Just make the kick fit the stroke." The best kick is usually one where all parts of the stroke simply harmonize to the eye. As the swimmer goes faster, the kick also speeds up. But remember: You don't swim faster just by kicking harder or faster. That will usually just waste energy, impede the development of a natural rhythm, and overwhelm the movement of the other parts of the stroke.

Butterfly Kicking

In the summer of 1999, Jenny Thompson swam 57.8 seconds for 100-meter butterfly to break the oldest world record in swimming and culminate an eight-year process of learning to swim butterfly the right way. It had been a relatively long haul. When she arrived at Stanford University as a freshman in the fall of 1991, she was already accomplished enough to have become one of the fastest of high school butterflyers. But she was certainly no threat to the world record. Just one year later she was so awesomely conditioned and powerful that she broke the world record in 100-meter freestyle, but she was still more than 3 seconds — a yawning gulf, by world-record standards — away from the butterfly mark.

And she might have stayed there, had Jenny not eventually learned one of the most important lessons in the stroke: to stop *kicking*. For while the Stanford women's team gets the cream of high school swimmers every year, Stanford Head Coach Richard Quick says that *every* freshman has to be taught not to *kick* in butterfly, at least not in the sense they're used to. What Jenny and all of her teammates learn is that butterfly kicking is really done with the core body, not the legs. By practicing short-axis rotation drills, first in a head-lead position (arms at the sides) and then in a hand-lead position (arms extended) they gradually learn to move efficiently through the water with rhythmic, effortless, body undulation. We call this motion body-dolphining, and we teach it through the drills described on pages 158-165 and shown on our video *BUTTERFLY AND BREASTSTROKE: The Total* Immersion *Way.*

As the body-dolphin movement begins to feel more natural through practice, you'll realize you are "kicking butterfly" *without* using your leg muscles. Simply by rhythmically pulsing your chest down and maintaining a long, supple bodyline, you create a body wave much like the ripple that flows through a garden hose when you snap one end. The "kick" is the last wave in that body dolphin, but the core body does most of the work.

After you have imprinted this new skill, you can begin doing short swims with the whole butterfly stroke. But the emphasis continues to be on rhythmically undulating the core body (initiated each time by pressing on the chest) and allowing the arms and legs to simply become extensions of core-body movement. The rhythm and power are in your core. When you want to move faster, you move your core faster.

I'll explain this process and how to train it in greater detail in the section on butterfly technique in Chapter 13. For now, the key point is that the butterfly kick is but one more example of how the job of the legs is primarily to integrate with core-body movement. In butterfly, as in the long-axis strokes, the legs are part of the kinetic chain when they're used properly, and the kinetic chain in turn takes the burden off the leg muscles and saves them from fatigue. Drills teach you the new movement habit of "not kicking." Then slow, controlled, fluent swimming integrates that habit into your whole-stroke and helps make it permanent.

Breaststroke Kicking

If you were hoping to find a place in swimming where the legs actually *do* have a starring role, you've found it. In all the other strokes, the pull creates more propulsion, more easily, than the kick ever could. In breaststroke, the reverse is true. And breaststroke kick is also somewhat less fully integrated with core-body rotation. I'll explain this more fully in the section on breaststroke technique in Chapter 13.

Considering strictly what part of the stroke makes you go forward, the breaststroke kick is a major part of the propulsion system — the body is moving faster at the end of the kick than it is at any other time in the stroke cycle. Because the body is moving faster, it is also encountering more drag than at any other time in the stroke cycle. So it's critically important to have everything forward of your hips streamlined into a needle-like position at the moment you complete your kick.

But there's one way in which the breaststroke kick is *not* an exception to the rule. When you want to swim faster in breaststroke, you do it by increasing the tempo of your short-axis rotation, not by kicking (or pulling) faster

How To Develop More Speed
Without Losing Fluency

B y now, it's obvious that TI swimmers do not speed up by pulling harder or faster, and they do not speed up by kicking harder or faster. Squeezing more speed out of yourself as you continue to swim fluently is a far more subtle and sophisticated process, but, once mastered, that knack is guaranteed to make you a much faster, more successful, and much happier swimmer. And that is one of the lessons — among many — you may find extremely difficult to learn while actually *swimming*. Sometimes, you can pick up what you need to know more easily through another sport.

Take the challenge of how to increase speed without losing fluency, without breaking the link between kinetic-chain power and our propelling movements. Our instinct to speed up by pulling and kicking faster is powerful. It is so powerful that, notwithstanding hundreds of pool lengths of drills or controlled-speed swimming to learn fluency, grace, and efficiency, the first time someone fires a starting gun, your hard-won efficiency may crumble into your old churning habits.

The best inoculation is a systematic plan to gradually expand the range of speeds and stroke rates at which you can swim smoothly, sometimes reaching out to another sport entirely to get the message across to your body. And the myriad things you can do to help your stroke, here are my three top s to speed:"

TI's Top Three Keys to Speed
Key #1: Train your torso.

Once you have learned the fundamentals of Fishlike Swimming, whether your swimming becomes raggedly choppy or remains fluidly graceful at higher speeds will be determined purely and simply by how you set your rhythm. Rhythm is just as important to a beautiful swimming stroke as it is to a beautifully performed piece of music. In the same way that a well-rehearsed orchestra plays in perfect harmony by taking its cues from the conductor, graceful and fluent swimming takes its cues from the core body. A bedrock principle of rhythmic movement is that timing and tempo should always originate at the center of the movement, not at the extremities. That's another way of saying that your arms and legs take their cues from the core, never the other way around. Two of my favorite non-swimming activities that can teach you this in no uncertain terms are cross-country skiing and in-line skating.

In both sports, the principle of propulsion is the same. While it seems, on the surface, that the energy pushing you forward comes from moving your legs, it's easy to prove this isn't so. For if you try to go faster by just moving your legs faster, you end up scrabbling them ineffectually, like a car spinning its wheels in sand. For the skier, the skater, and, for that matter, the car, the secret to power and propulsion is traction. You must anchor your foot (there's that kinetic chain concept again!) before you push off. Cross-country skis are bowed in the middle; that mid-section must be weighted and pressed into the snow to get a grip. After gliding forward on your right foot, you must put *all* of your weight on it to gain traction. Only then can you push off with it and thrust the left leg forward. In-line skating works in much the same way.

Thus in both sports, your speed (or stride rate) is determined not by how fast you can move your legs but by how fast you can *shift your weight*. Try to move your legs faster than you can shift your weight and you lose your anchor, your power, and ultimately your forward momentum. Your stride rate may increase, but your stride length — how far you travel each time you thrust a leg forward — will deteriorate precipitously, and your fluency and efficiency will go right along with it. The only thing that will happen faster is the rate which you fatigue.

Swimming works the same way. Trying to swim faster by moving arms faster is a quick route to a ragged, exhausting stroke...for two First, arms that move too fast cut themselves adrift from the torso energy. Compared to the torso, the arms have relatively little mass accelerate them much more rapidly than you can your core body. If your torso is unable to match the rhythm of your arms, the torso simply drops out. This is like sitting on a playground swing and pumping your legs rapidly without using your upper body. Second, as we discussed earlier, if the armstroke rate gets too high, you can't anchor your hand. You lose your grip just as surely as you lose your traction in skating and skiing when your legs move faster than you can shift your weight. The result is similar, too: You take shorter strokes. You take *more* strokes per lap, which causes fatigue. Your hand slips instead of anchors. You lose power.

Again — just as in skating and skiing — you swim fast efficiently by using weight shifts to set your tempo. Speed up in freestyle and backstroke by shifting your weight faster from side to side. As you move your torso faster, stay balanced and "swim downhill" (leaning on your chest in freestyle or your upper back in backstroke). In butterfly and breaststroke, rock your hips and shoulders faster and you can't *help* but go faster. In breaststroke, for example, when you drive your chest down and forward faster after the breath, you also drive your hands forward to their anchoring point faster and you drive your hips *up* faster, setting you up more quickly for the next powerful core-body contraction that brings your hips to your hands' anchoring point.

Key #2: Limit your stroke count.

It can't be repeated too often: It's to be expected that your stroke count will go up a bit as you go faster. But a *dramatic* increase in your stroke count as you go faster usually means that you're giving up too much efficiency (*i.e.*, stroke length) for your increased speed. As your stroke efficiency improves, as we said in Chapter 2, you'll see two changes in stroke count. First, your stroke-count range (the span from the lowest count you can possibly achieve at "super-slow" swimming speeds to the count it takes to swim at your fastest speed) will move lower. Second, that same range will get narrower.

I speak from experience. The lowest 25-yard stroke count I could man-
≥ 30 years ago in college was about 14 strokes per length. At racing speeds,
⁀atigued, that might balloon up to 26. Today, even though I'm no longer
hailing distance of college age, my lowest stroke count (at super-slow
speeds) is 8 strokes per length and at race speed, 16 or 17. That's
⌐ver the past three decades, I've worked tirelessly and intensively
⁀ficiency. My stroke-count range has dropped at both ends, with
'ling by six strokes and the "ceiling" falling by nine. And the range

has narrowed from 12, to 8 or 9.

Your range in short-axis strokes should be much narrower than in long-axis strokes. The best male sprinter I coached at West Point had a freestyle range of 7 strokes — from 6 s/l when he was practicing super-slow swimming, to a racing maximum of 13 s/l. As a butterflyer his range was only 3 strokes — from 5 s/l at maximum efficiency and minimum speed, to a maximum of 8 s/l when racing 100 yards.

Your own ability to stay fluent at your full range of speeds from super slow to racing can be measured the same way: finding how close you can bring your "floor" and your "ceiling" together. Check that now by swimming a pool length at your slowest speed with your longest possible stroke. After resting a bit, swim another at your absolute maximum speed. Don't try to swim in any special way: *Just go fast.* How much difference is there between the two counts? Good. Now start reducing the gap between the two. Both skill work and simply making it a habit to count *every* length you swim will help you reach your goal.

Key #3: Know when to slow down.

Knowing when to slow down is more important than almost anything else when it comes to learning to swim fast fluently. I can relate endless stories about great sprinters who spent an astonishing amount of time swimming slowly. In 1981-82, for example, I coached a University of Virginia grad named Phil Perdue who had continued training and competing after college. Despite having to fit in training around a full-time job, he achieved a world ranking of 10th and 11th in the 50-meter free for the two years I worked with him. Phil would arrive late to practice each day after work. He would then swim with incredible ease, beauty, and precision for 15 minutes before gradually increasing his speed but losing none of the silky quality of his super-slow swimming. There was a seamless connection between the way he looked when swimming slowly and how he looked at full speed. Phil instinctively kn how to use "slow" to improve "fast." It's a skill the rest of us can develop

While coaching the sprinters at West Point, I spent far more time a ishing them to slow down than to swim faster. The non-negotiable r "You can swim only as fast as you can swim with fluency and cc instant you feel your stroke becoming rough or you feel yourse⌐ struggle,' you're to slow down."

I paid much more attention to the flow of their strokes t'

clock or my stopwatch. One day in the fall of 1998, I had the sprint group practicing a series of 50-meter repeats on which they were to swim the first 6 stroke cycles (approximately 20 meters) at maximum speed and SR, then swim slowly the rest of the length. The two best sprinters, Joe Novak and Heidi Borden, were swimming with impeccable flow. Even at maximum speed, there was total coordination between their limbs and torso. But a plebe named Scott Edwards was choppy and ineffective. In trying to maximize his SR, he shortened his stroke and flattened his body roll.

I called Scott up on deck to watch Joe and Heidi for several minutes, to observe how they kept a long stroke and ideal body roll in a nearly seamless manner even at high SR. I then explained that he shouldn't be surprised if it took him his entire first season to learn that kind of coordination, and that the way to learn it was to *first* establish the desired SL and core-body action, *then* raise his SR as high as he could while still maintaining fluency, and no higher. The exciting thing was that practically as soon as he slowed down, Scott's core body integration with arms and legs became nearly perfect, and all at once each stroke expressed grace and power — far more power, in fact.

Of course, the difficulty of maintaining fluency at faster speeds is far greater for sprinters, who must prepare themselves to race at much higher stroke rates. But the challenge is the same for all of us. Whatever speed and stroke rate *you* will use when racing, you must first learn how to maintain control, fluency, and a long stroke at every point on the speed/stroke-rate curve between super slow and maximum.

And that means being smart enough to realize that to go really fast, you first have to know when to slow down.

Drills: How Theory Becomes Practice
(And How You Become a Better Swimmer)

E nough talk. Having read this far, you could probably give a convincing chalkboard lecture of your own on how to become a more fishlike swimmer. So it's time to roll up our sleeves (if swimmers had any) and get into the pool. It's time to *learn how to learn* the skills you need to master.

But first a caveat: The skills that will make you more of a fish won't come naturally. You'll need to make a conscious, diligent, and attentive effort to begin "imprinting" them and, over time, to make them as instinctive as the wasteful and tiring habits they'll replace. The good news is that "diligent" doesn't mean "difficult." In fact, the steps you'll be following are so simple that virtually anyone can do them. And the process will be far more rewarding and enjoyable than any conventional lap or training routine you have ever experienced.

Most everything you need to master is contained in the series of TI Lessons that begin on page 98. These lessons are designed to help you build each stroke from the ground up, using easily mastered drills. We'll help you break each stroke into bite-sized bits that you master individually, then gradually assemble into a whole new way of moving. Each step is easy to work on, so you're practicing success, not failure. It's a virtually guaranteed process that is:

1. **Flexible.** You can choose just the right degree of drill difficulty and continually adjust it to provide an appropriate challenge.
2. **Sequential.** Each step provides precisely the skill or awareness you'll need to tackle the step that follows.
3. **Incremental.** Each step is slightly more advanced than the previous one.

And there are no wasted moves. *Every* drill teaches you an ingredient essential to the fluency and skill that will make you fishlike in the whole stroke. When that finally happens, you'll not only swim better, but also enjoy it more. In fact, you will feel good *every* time you swim. And the ongoing challenge of becoming increasingly fluent will make swimming just as satisfying mentally as it is physically. On top of that, you will be prepared to take over as your own coach, to continue refining your efficiency more and more and more — practically forever.

For us to help you succeed in all this, however, we need to do more than teach efficient stroking. We need to teach you how to create and sustain what we like to call a swimming "flow state," an almost euphoric condition similar to the famous runner's high in which you virtually lose yourself in the satisfaction of an activity. What gets you into that flow state? Doing something that you value, that brings you pleasure, that requires concentration, and that provides a feeling of competency and mastery. And it's the "drill pieces," pieces that will gradually come together as your new stroke, that can best put you on the "flow state" path.

Learning vs. Just Training

Total Immersion has outperformed all other swim-improvement methods because it teaches skills the way we learn them best — in small, logically organized pieces. Learning any new motor skill is a problem-solving, trial-and-error exercise. But *too much* error can be so discouraging that enthusiasm goes right down the drain, and with it the chance to improve.

The secret is to practice something you *can* do, not something you can't. That means first breaking a complex or advanced skill into simple tasks that can easily and quickly be mastered, then recombining those tasks gradually, seamlessly, and effortlessly into an integrated whole. Each basic task becomes the springboard for a more advanced one, and that is exactly what our TI swim lessons do.

Makes perfect sense, don't you think? Well then, why do so few swimming coaches teach this way? Because they spend so much time training athletes, and so little time teaching, that few have thought about how to break down the complex skills of swimming into a series of simpler mini tasks. Because they coach in the "whole-stroke" world, their advice typically comes in scattershot bursts as they spot something wrong and try to tell you how to fix that one thing. . . and then the next thing. . . and then the next thing, kind of like putting a bunch of Band-Aids on a gaping wound. Instead, we offer a logical series of "success lessons" that are mastered quickly, and that lay the groundwork for higher-level skills that gradually crystallize into a well-formed stroke that doesn't need "spot fixing."

The swimmer's instinctive conviction that whole-stroke swimming is the path to *better* whole-stroke swimming is also to blame for this wrong-headed approach. Far too many of us, coached and uncoached, hamper our own learning by spending too much time swimming the whole stroke without first achieving real fluency in its fundamental parts. Whole-stroke swimming, for most people, is time spent "practicing how to struggle." To learn a better way of swimming you have to actively unlearn the style you're stuck with, which means *never doing it again*. Every length you swim with poor form makes it that much harder to change to a smoother form.

In a sense, TI drills will help you reach your goal in a more direct way than the route taken by some of the world's best swimmers — the ones whose fluency and effortlessness make it all look so natural. While these human fish have had coaches who helped them to where they are today, they have also had to rely even more heavily on their exceptional "body intuition" to know when they had it right. They've experienced countless breakthrough moments when their stroke has felt just right, moments that the kinesthetically gifted swimmer can immediately seize and store in a catalogue of similar "how-to move" experiences. Eventually, an elite swimmer's skill library becomes cc prehensive enough to produce an extremely smooth and highly efficie of swimming.

But this process takes too long and, unless you are kinesthe and have unlimited time, it's a process that won't happen for y TI steps in, takes this somewhat haphazard and slow proces for you. With our step-by-step drill system, any swimmer ca own flashes of insight, store them in muscle memory, an an organized, convenient, and reliable way, instead o now and again by accident. And by practicing the m nts become more natural, automatic, and in

Eventually, when you do go back to swimming after polishing the pieces of it in your drills, your body re-assembles the stroke naturally into a much-improved whole. Your nervous system has taken so many "snapshots" of sensations similar to the ones the elite swimmers instinctively feel, that it becomes easy for you to assemble them into a complete "movie." And because our natural efficiency in water is so limited to start with, bettering it is a process that never really ends. One of the most exciting things about swimming is that there's virtually no "improvement ceiling" when it comes to good technique. Whether you're a beginner learning basics or an elite looking to medal at a national meet, there's always something new to work on.

Natural Learning: Experience Is the Best Teacher

As children, each of us learned essential land-based life skills such as how to move, balance, lift, climb, and carry, without any formal instruction. But as adults, natural learning rarely happens for us in water because we seldom feel truly comfortable there, and because swimming instruction is usually presented in ways that actually hinder natural learning. Our TI drill progressions fix that, taking you back in a way to the easy naturalness of childhood experience. They guide you through a series of exercises that let you discover how your body behaves in the water and reveal how to use that awareness to fullest advantage. The process is systematic, as we've said, but it's not rigid; think of these drills as a liberating opportunity to discover fluency on your own.

The drill process transforms your swimming most completely when you free yourself from the pressure to swim "right" or to go fast. Experiment with each exercise for as long as you want, repeating it as many times as you want. Your goal is not some sort of strict perfection, but relaxation and fluidity; to dually turn each exercise from unfamiliar and possibly a little awkward, smooth and easy.

erstand that, once you begin, the toughest thing to overcome will no our stroke but your impatience. We've learned through teaching to thousands of swimmers that after a few days of practicing o worry that they're not doing enough *work* to stay in shape. drills to be a quick fix that lets them get back to their ailing her than a completely new way to practice swimming.

e stand in your way. Know what every smart athlete aste *always* pays greater dividends than increasing u'll become a much better swimmer if you allow

A DOSE OF DRILLS

They're the best medicine for your stroke because . . .

1. **Your swimming muscles need a shot of amnesia.** If you've been struggling with your stroke for months or even years, your muscles have become very good at moving inefficiently. And they will happily keep it up for as long as you keep swimming. Stroke drills can break that cycle because they're so different from your normal motion that your muscles don't "recognize" the movement. Result: You can finally practice new movement patterns on a neuromuscular "blank slate."

2. **Small pieces are easier to swallow.** Because the swimming stroke is made up of so many finely coordinated parts, it's virtually impossible to digest the whole thing. So our Total Immersion drills break down the stroke into a series of easily mastered mini skills, presented in logical order. Each drill teaches a key skill, and mastery of each step gives you the key to mastering the next one. You simply assemble these "building blocks" into a new, more efficient stroke.

3. **"Trial and success" outperforms trial and error.** "Mini skills" can be mastered quickly and easily. So from the very first lap you begin programming yourself for smooth movements, and erasing your "struggling skills." The more you practice fluency and control, and the more they become your new movement habit, the faster you learn to swim better. That string of successes boosts your motivation and self-confidence — and studies have shown that learning happens faster when you feel good about what you're doing.

4. **Skill drills are self-adjusting.** The more you need them, the more drills help you. Beginners learn basic skills in big chunks, and rough edges get smoothed off quickly. Experienced swimmers, doing the same drills, tune in naturally to far more subtle refinements, bringing a higher degree of polish to skills they already have. And the more you have to learn, the more you should drill -- up to four times as much as your "normal" swimming if you're a novice. (In butterfly, it's actually better not to do *any* whole-stroke swimming early in the learning process.)

Bottom line? Less swimming and more drills will make you a better swimmer, faster, than any other training program — even though it means you'll log less distance per hour of swimming.

yourself the freedom to swim with a sense of exploration and discovery, rather than with your usual sense of determination or obligation. If you are to master swimming as an art, you can't treat the water as just another piece of exercise equipment. As your skill improves, you'll be able to do more swimming and more "training," but every stroke and lap will be far more productive and effective.

This goes double, by the way, for anyone who swims competitively. Learning is about change, and the competitive attitude often resists that. Yes there is risk in shifting your focus away from speed and effort, but the reward is proportionate to the risk. If you *fail* to change, if you continue to do everything just as you always have, how can you expect to improve any faster than before? Where will anything but the usual fractional performance improvements come from?

For this learning experience to be successful, there must be not just change, but big change — not only in the way you swim, but also in your very thinking about swimming and the importance you give to the component parts of the experience. This is nothing less than what's now commonly called a "paradigm shift." Where previously it might have seemed vital to test your capacity for hard work, you might now consider it equally important to sometimes explore how *easily* you can do something. Where previously you might have felt it important to kick as hard as possible when swimming fast, now you might strive to make sure your legs are integrating naturally and easily with what your entire body is doing. Swimming is no longer about brute strength but about sheer smarts.

The drills work best if you allow yourself to "play" in a free, unstructured way before channeling your developing new relationship with the water into formal swimming. And, most important, get in the habit of *feeling* more. What subtle errors in your stroke make swimming harder? What equally subtle corrections make it easier? What movements or positions increase the water's resistance, and what adjustments make you more slippery? What habits make you feel more ragged, and which changes make you feel smooth? You will discover none of this so long as you keep doing the same old laps, just trying to keep up with the pace clock or other swimmers. But patient, attentive drill practice will reveal insights like this *on every length*. Your senses will tell you how you're doing. What *feels* right, usually *is* right.

HOW TO MAKE EVERY MINUTE OF DRILL PRACTICE COUNT

I've said over and over that drills work better than anything else for making significant changes (improvements!) in your swimming. Want to get *all* the value out of every minute of practice? Follow a few simple guidelines:

Keep your focus narrow. Do just one thing well. Even though the simplest drills still have three to five "bullet points," pay attention to only one point on each repeat, particularly when first learning the drill. Once you feel confident you're doing it well (and it no longer requires *all* of your brainpower to do so), shift your focus to the next. After the various points begin to feel more natural, you can begin thinking about two, then three, at once.

Make repeats short. When teaching drills in workshops, we never have the class go more than 25 yards before stopping for feedback. Follow this simple rule: Don't continue a drill beyond the point where you feel it's going well. Why practice even a little inefficiency? Instead, take a break, regroup, then resume.

Keep sets brief. Long sets produce fatigue and fatigue mars your execution and blurs your focus. Stay with one drill or one focal point for no longer than 10 minutes, then try integrating that focus in some whole-stroke practice, or switch to a different drill focus.

Rest. Many coaches put drills on challenging intervals, either to boost yards-per-minute or to test their swimmers' toughness. What they're more likely achieving is ragged drill execution, which makes the entire exercise pointless. Take all the rest you need. Make each repetition as good as — or better than — the first. Besides, if you're genuinely focused on ease and economy, your heart rate will stay in the aerobic range and you won't need much recovery between reps in the first place.

One way to eliminate interval pressure is to rest for a given number of deep, slow breaths — between three and five is about right. That will not only provide enough rest but also relax and center you for better execution on the next rep.

But however long you rest, take at least enough time to evaluate your last rep and plan how to improve the next one.

Focus on mechanics, then feelings. When learning a new drill, focus first on getting the basic movements, coordination, and timing right. Once you've done that, begin working on the *qualities* of fishlike swimming in the drill, qualities such as comfort, relaxation, economy, silence, "feeling like a needle slipping through a small hole," etc. When you switch from drilling to swimming, vary your focus in the same way, sometimes keying in on specific movements, other times focusing on general sensations.

Have patience. Spend *all the time necessary* to master each step. Hurrying means a greater chance of practicing inefficiency — and continuing to waste your hard-won energy when you swim. This is particularly true for the balance drills for both long-axis and short-axis skills.

Take the pledge. Repeat this to yourself: "A drill done 100% right is 100% right. A drill done 99% right is 100% wrong."

When you practice every part of a drill as it's designed, you learn efficient, fluent, satisfying movement. When you're off by even a little bit (not hitting your "sweet spot," missing on the timing, over-kicking, not feeling ease or control, etc.) you're forced into some kind of compensation — lifting your head, arching your back, using your arms as support levers, and the like. Those bad habits then make their way into your swimming and eventually become a permanent part of your stroke.

Practice doesn't make perfect; it only makes permanent whatever you happen to be practicing!

Drill Practice for Every Swimmer: Novice to Champ

The great genius of drills, remember, is that they're self-adjusting. The same drill that teaches basic movement to a beginner can burnish subtle refinement into an advanced swimmer's stroke. As a result, each ability level, from novice to Olympic hopeful, follows its own drill "recipe," benefiting most from a relatively custom drill plan: how much drilling vs. swimming; how much work on basic balance vs. more advanced drills; how and when to integrate drilling and swimming; etc. As you'll see in the guidelines below, it's far more than just "beginners need the most drills and experts need the least." Drills, remember, are stroke-builders in the beginning, and stroke-polishers later on. Here are some general principles for when you as an individual should use them, and when you can safely put them away.

Novice Swimmers

If you are new to swimming — say a runner who's eyeing that first triathlon, or growing fed up with knee injuries and looking for a new sport — I often advise doing little to no whole-stroke swimming until you've mastered simpler movements or mini skills, particularly the pertinent balance skills for the stroke you're learning. That goes too for swimmers who've been at it a while but have had little coaching (or who, despite years of laps, have never acquired much skill), or who are learning a new or difficult stroke (butterfly is a good example). If you came to one of our TI workshops, we'd teach you just as we teach non-swimming kids or adults, doing *nothing else* until you had mastered Supine Balance, the first drill in our first lesson. Then you would patiently advance through the other static head-lead balance drills, before attempting any active head-lead balance drills. And so on.

If you're coaching or teaching yourself, simply follow the same principle. Imperfect balance at step one, or any shaky fundamental at any subsequent step, means you'll employ (memorize!) some form of compensating movement to correct it. That imprints inefficiency. Don't do it.

How much drilling? Probably 70% to 100% of your total swimming yardage. Your entire emphasis should be on learning skilled movement. As for conditioning, for now that's "something that happens to you while you practice your skills" as we're fond of saying at TI. If you're chronically worried about whether you're staying in shape, either condition yourself with a stroke different from the one you're working on or, better yet, when practice is over just get out of the pool and head for the gym.

What drills, when? Just follow the lesson plans we've outlined in the Lessons section, and the advice in the drill guidelines above. Also, you'll find additional guidance, and suggested practice schedules, on the Total Immersion Virtual Team page of the www.swimware.com web site.

What to do when you swim? Swim only as long/far/fast as your whole-stroke holds together perfectly. That means for as long as it feels as smooth, as controlled, and just plain as good, as your drills feel. Focus on one of the bullet points you were practicing in the drill, such as hiding your head or swimming downhill; or count your strokes; or just evaluate how you feel overall. The instant you start to detect even a little raggedness, stop swimming and go back to drilling.

Avoid timed repeats on intervals in the stroke you are learning, at least until you can keep the stroke count — or your ease and smoothness, certainly — consistent for at least 10 minutes of relaxed, slow (short!) repeats. Repeats, in fact, should never last any longer than your ability to do them efficiently and easily.

Intermediate Swimmers

If you're in this tent, you have lots of company. Perhaps you swam competitively 10 or 20 years ago but never quite got past "middling." Or you did better than that, but it's been a long time since your last race and you know technique has changed a lot since then. Or, maybe you're a triathlete with some good swim-training experience who already races in the upper half of the swim pack, but just knows you could run *and* bike much faster if swimming took less of your energy. Or maybe you're an active competitive swimmer with lots of headroom for learning and improvement — whole-stroke swimming at moderate speeds is a piece of cake for you, but pick up the pace and your efficiency evaporates. In each case, you'll reach your goals much more quickly by trading some "training" for concentrated *practice*.

How much drilling? Anywhere from 40% to 100% of your overall yardage. The percentage should be up to 100% if you:

• have just returned to swimming after a year-long "retirement"
• have finally decided to put a major emphasis on becoming efficient after years of generic, unfocused lap swimming or workouts
• are working on a new stroke
• are beginning a new competitive swim season.

Trim that to 80% when your new drills feel 100% right, by beginning to integrate some whole-stroke swimming in the way recommended for novices. (An 80:20 mix of drill:swim is also good for any 8-and-under age-group swimmer or novice competitive swimmer.)

Reduce the drill component to 60% — and no further — only when your stroke is good enough to "take off the training wheels." That means you can swim sets of no-drilling, moderate-speed, moderate-distance, moderate-rest repeats with consistent stroke counts and form. A 60:40 mix of drill:swim is also good for a competitive swimmer of intermediate skill in mid-season, and for any age-group swimmer age 10 years or under.

You can mix drills with swimming in a 40:60 ratio when you are able to swim timed sets, descending sets, etc., on somewhat more difficult intervals while maintaining a consistent stroke count, and can effectively "trade" strokes for speed (*i.e.*, control the increase in your s/l and stay smooth and fluent when you increase your speed). This ratio is also good for competitive swimmers of moderately advanced skill in mid-season, or age group swimmers of age 11 to 13 years.

What drills when? Do all-drill sets whenever you are working intensively on skill improvement or learning something new. Follow our lesson plans in the Lessons section when you do. Do sets, alternating drill and swim, when trying to transfer the new skill or awareness to your stroke. Use either drill or drill-swim sets as warmup and recovery, or in place of kickboard training when you are shifting your emphasis from learning to training.

What to do when you swim? As an intermediate swimmer your skills are still relatively unformed and your "swimming intuition" has a good way to go. You need to be very diligent about not "practicing inefficiency" in training (unless of course you really don't want to become the best swimmer you can be).

So, most of your whole-stroke swimming should still be focused on maintaining consistent stroke counts or on making the drills' focal points feel more natural when you're swimming. You can also test yourself with some descending or faster swims, occasionally simulating the pace or effort of your races. For these sets, choose repeat distances long enough to allow you to feel the speed and power you'd like while racing, but not so long that you begin to grow ragged. A good general guide when you're simulating race pace, tempo, or effort, is repeat distances of 10% to 25% of the race distance. And one thing more: Keep your top practice speed down to "easy speed" instead of "all-out speed." Testing your ability to push through the pain will mainly prove that your form won't hold up to the stress.

Advanced Swimmers

Even advanced swimmers — up to and including world record holders — can still benefit from focused drill practice. Why? Because the more elite the competition, the more likely that places, records, and qualifying times are determined by tiny margins. And the closer you get to a world record, the tougher those tenths and hundredths of seconds become to shave off. Any advantage pays. Besides that, the faster you go, the harder it is to overpower the drag resisting your body — and drag reduction is built into nearly every TI drill. Finally, even if you are an Olympic swimmer or world champion — the absolute *best* in your event — your energy efficiency is still less than 10% and, like the rest of us, you can make easier gains by reducing energy waste than by increasing energy supply.

How much drilling?

- 80% to 100% if you are correcting a stubborn glitch in a particular stroke; or are beginning a new season; or need intensive restoration after illness or a particularly intensive workout or training phase; or are rehabilitating after a swimming injury (and want to correct the technique errors that almost certainly contributed to that injury in the first place). Highly focused and purposeful drill practice is always better than "garbage yardage" in any kind of recovery workout.

- 40% to 70% when you're putting an extra focus on efficiency, are doing basic aerobic conditioning or early season gradual buildup, need general recovery from hard training, or are in an off-season maintenance-training and foundation-improving stage.

- 10% to 30% as a routine base level of drill/technique work; during warmups for any practice or meet; as preparation for an important main set; as recovery between sets or as the "easy" part of fartlek (easy/fast) training; as a far more beneficial alternative to kickboard sets; but *never* as intensive training.

What drills when? Even an élite swimmer can benefit enormously from working on the most basic balance drills, as Jenny Thompson discovered during her quest to break the world record in the 100-meter butterfly (see pages 74-75). So use the entire sequence of drills in a particular lesson, or for a particular stroke, including the common-axis drills for that stroke (*i.e.,* backstroke drills for a freestyler, or butterfly drills for a breaststroker).

The basic drills can also be a routine element of everyday parts of your practice, such as warmup. Think of it as similar to the way an accomplished musician still practices scales backstage to limber up for a performance "out front."

In early season, practice drills from all the strokes to improve your general library of motor skills for fishlike swimming. Learning (or re-learning) to move more fluently in all strokes will unquestionably help increase your efficiency in any one stroke. Just follow the carefully chosen and proven-to-be-effective sequences in our lesson plans. For your primary stroke or event, identify specific drill sequences that you know help put your stroke in a particularly good groove. Use these before important sets, or during your meet warmup.

Choose active balance drills from Lessons Two and Three as a useful alternative to low-value kickboard sets.

And when using drills as recovery between sets or between harder re-peats during a set, you may get even more complete recovery by doing drills from a different stroke. Use drills from the same stroke as your recovery if you need a technique refresher to set you up to stay controlled on the next hard swim. Use drills from another stroke if you mainly need more physical recovery.

What to do when you swim? As an accomplished swimmer, you should be able to do the entire range of swimming repeats, all distances and all inten-sities, in training without significant breakdowns in efficiency. But just to be certain you keep your focus on s/l when swimming fast, make stroke count-ing a habit, and strive to do an ever-improving job of adding the fewest strokes possible as you go faster, or increasing your ability to swim fast at any given stroke count.

At this point, you've probably heard just about all you want to hear about the value of drills. But the good news is that the classroom part is now offi-cially over. It's time to take these "building blocks" that will eventually be-come your new and improved stroke, and begin putting them together. As the notice on some products cautions, "some assembly is required." Same thing goes for changing drills into real swimming. So, turn the page and let's discover how to finally fit together the pieces of the puzzle.

Part 2

The Total Immersion Drill Progressions

Chapter 11

How to Use the Drill Progressions for Maximum Benefit

This book describes the drills taught by Total Immersion as of the year 2000. These drills are extremely effective, and will help you learn to swim better than you ever thought possible. We *strongly* recommend, however, that you use this book in conjunction with our two videos.

As effective as the descriptions on the following pages are, you will gain a much more complete understanding of the movements of each of these drills by watching them being demonstrated on the videos. You will learn physical skills far more quickly, easily, and completely with visual aids than by trying to follow written descriptions in a book. To gain maximum benefit from this book, we recommend that you use the videos to learn the drills, and use this book to learn the principles behind the drills and the concept of fishlike swimming. The two products will complement each other – and your swimming.

An additional useful tool is the 26-page waterproof *POOL PRIMER for FREESTYLE AND BACKSTROKE*. The primer distills and illustrates the key points of all the freestyle and backstroke drills shown on the freestyle/backstroke video. It also helps you troubleshoot the common problems you may experience in mastering each drill. The *POOL PRIMER* can be taken with you to the pool deck as a visual reference tool for the long-axis drills.

To order the videos, *POOL PRIMER*, or any of our other products, please visit our website at www.totalimmersion.net or call us at 800-609-7946. You may also mail or fax us the order form on page 207 of this book.

Long-Axis Drill Progressions

Lesson One: Learn Basic Balance with Head-Lead Drills

We always start teaching and stroke refinement with head-lead drills, in which you hold your arms lightly at your sides. Even if you feel you already have efficient strokes, if you've never practiced these drills before, *start here.* These are the drills that most quickly give you the most critical gift of balance – the knowledge of how to get the water to support you. Once you do that, all of your movements will be more relaxed, more natural, and less inhibited.

Head-lead drills are critical to this process because for most swimmers, the tendency to use the arms as stabilizers – just as you might instinctively reach out for a wall while standing on one leg – will be powerful. Until you learn to fully master balance using only your head and core body, you will have a difficult time using your arms only to lengthen your body and hold on to the water as you propel with the kinetic chain. Because you cannot use your arms for support in head-lead drills, they teach you the purest sense of balance. They are also effective in creating greater self awareness because, without your arms extended, you'll know immediately if your head, neck, and torso are out of alignment or are moving incorrectly.

*Most swimmers tend to use their arms as stabilizers –
especially when they need to take a breath.*

General guidelines for head-lead drills include:

1. Practice for very short repeats – 25 yards or less – until they become "no brainers."
2. Try to master them without the aid of fins; the "fin effect" will tend to be too magnified when you don't have an arm extended.
3. Put no emphasis on speed in practicing head-lead drills. Your most important objectives are to do them easily, gently, silently, and with a sense of stillness. Of all the TI drills, these are probably the closest to a "Zen experience."

Drill #1.1: Basic Balance: Supine (On Your Back)

Why do this drill: This is the easiest way to learn ease and relaxation. Without the distraction of having to breathe, you can more easily learn how to get the water to support you. That sense of *effortless support, stillness, and stability* is the key sensation associated with balance; in subsequent drills we'll take it to other positions.

Follow this sequence:

1. Hide your head. Ears under the surface and only your face showing above it. Face parallel to the surface.

2. Lean on your upper back until your hips feel light and you feel totally supported by the water. A "dry patch of thigh" should clear the water with each kick.

3. Keep your flutter kick compact and silent, with your knees and toes submerged.

4. The test of true balance is being able to *do nothing* with your arms. If you feel as if you need to use your arms to "brace" yourself or scull, then you aren't balanced.

5. Just lie there, kicking gently and letting the water do the work. ***This feeling is the essence of how balance feels!*** Maintain this feeling in the other balance drills.

Drill #1.2: Basic Balance: Prone (On Your Stomach)

Why do this drill: You won't swim freestyle in exactly this position (you'll be rolling, not flat), but this does show you how easy it is to get the water to support you effortlessly when you keep your head and neck aligned and shift your weight forward. It also gives a dramatic lesson in what happens to your balance when you lift your head.

Follow this sequence:

1. Look directly at the bottom. You shouldn't see anything ahead of you.

2. Hide your head (just a sliver of the back of your head should show above the surface). Feel as if any wavelet could wash over the back of your head.

3. Kick with a compact, quiet, gentle flutter. The lazier the better. Moving quickly is not important at all. Balance – feeling supported by the water – is primary.

4. Lean on your chest until your hips float freely. (Don't try to hold them up; release them to the surface.) Ask someone to watch; they should see your suit just brush the surface. If they see an inch or more of "cheeks" above the surface, you're pressing too much. If they see an inch or more of water covering them, you're not pressing enough. Your hips should also rock gently back and forth as you kick; they shouldn't be locked in place.

5. Breathing forward upsets your balance, so you have two goals. Keep your kick so lazy that you don't have to breathe very often; this allows you to focus on feeling stable. Second, breathe with as little fuss or upset as possible, then rebalance after each breath.

    Advance to the next drill when: You're relaxed, stable, and flowing with a sense that the water is doing most of the work and your gentle kicking is going entirely into propulsion, not into helping keep your legs afloat.

Drill #1.3 : Basic Balance: Side (Looking Down)

Why do this drill: You'll swim both long-axis strokes more on your side than on your chest or back. Now that you know how it feels to be balanced and supported, you'll try to get that same feeling on your side.

Follow this sequence:

1. Lie on one side, looking directly down. Your hip and shoulder point directly at the ceiling. Keep your head "hidden" — exactly as it felt in Drill #1.2.

2. Lean on your shoulder until your top arm is "dry" from shoulder to fingertips. You should feel air on your arm.

3. Kick from the top of your thigh and focus on keeping your bodyline long from hip to toes, but *don't* put much effort into pointing your toes.

4. ***Slip your body through the smallest possible "hole" in the water.***
   Try to lengthen your line from head to toes and shape your body like a
   torpedo, arms hugging your sides.

5. To breathe, swivel your head to nose-up and roll back enough so that
   you can get air easily. Keep feeling like a long, balanced needle as you
   breathe, then return to the nose-down position.

6. When learning, practice for short distances so that you don't need to
   breathe more than once or twice. When you do need to breathe, just

swivel your head from a nose-down to a nose-up position and roll back enough so that you can get air easily. Keep your head "hidden" as you breathe.

Advance to the next drill when: You feel comfortable and supported on either side. You should be able to balance and *do nothing* with either arm. The "dry" arm simply lies on your side; the "wet" arm hugs your lower side. Finally you should feel as if your kick moves you more easily and efficiently in this more slippery side-balance position.

Drill #1.4: Find Your Sweet Spot

Why do this drill: The Sweet Spot is your true side-balance position for all long-axis drills. The Sweet Spot is completely individual and almost never exactly on the side – the nose-down drill above excepted. Virtually all swimmers do "side balance" better in a position somewhat on the back. Mastering it is important because you'll start and finish every long-axis drill here. If you learn your Sweet Spot, you'll practice your drills with ease and fluency; if you don't, it means tension and struggle.

Follow this sequence:

1. Start as in Drill #1.3, balanced on your side, looking directly down, kicking easily with a long leg, and with your body shaped like a long, balanced needle.

2. When you feel balanced (head hidden, arm showing), swivel your head and roll back until you can breathe easily, then stay there for the rest of the length.

3. If you don't feel *great*, roll another 5 or 10 degrees onto your back, until you feel more comfortable and are able to keep your needle shape.
4. Once you feel balanced, practice **slipping your body through the smallest hole in the water.**
5. Focus on stillness. Imagine carrying a champagne glass on your forehead or shoulder.

6. Practice on both sides. You may not feel equally comfortable on both
    sides, but work mindfully at balance on both sides until you feel as re-
    laxed as possible on each.

Practice Tips for Lesson One

This completes Lesson One – Basic Balance. All of your practice in this
lesson should be at the easiest possible effort level until balance is almost
automatic. Additionally, you should do about 90% of all Lesson-One drill practice in repeats of 25 yards or less, at least until you have achieved mastery of
all the objectives outlined for the four drills above.

Two practice-planning ideas can be helpful in keeping your focus on *how
well* you practice, rather than on *how much* or *how fast*. Rather than aiming
for a certain number of yards in a practice, or number of repeats in a set, take
more of a Zen approach. Practice mindfully for as long you feel fluent and
controlled or for as long as it takes to get a sense that the movement is becoming "grooved." Alternately, you can practice for a given period of time, say
60 minutes, broken into 6 blocks of 10 minutes. Then do whatever number of
repeats you complete in 10 minutes, before moving on to the next item in
your practice.

For rest intervals, instead of using the pace clock, take a certain number
of deep, cleansing breaths (or bobs, with your head sinking just under the
surface after each in-breath) between the time you reach the wall and when

you push off again. If I'm practicing 25s with great ease, I find that two to three cleansing breaths are ample recovery. If I do 50s or 75s, I might take four to five breaths before pushing off again.

And finally, your kinesthetic feedback should include your sense of how gently, silently, bubble-free, and splash-free you can make your practice. Once you have a good sense of doing the mechanics well, shift your attention to what your other senses are telling you.

Vertical Kicking (VK)

When you practice long-axis drills for the first time, you'll discover that you need at least a moderate flutter kick to do the drills reasonably well. But at workshops we always emphasize that the kick should be incidental. The primary objective of Lessons One and Two is to improve your balance to the point where you can swim quite well with very little kicking.

The main contribution of your kick to long-axis drills is in maintaining some flow or momentum during the pauses that are integral to each drill. If you're not getting at least a bit of propulsion from your legs, your body simply stops moving, and drilling becomes a tiring, lurching affair. It's far easier to keep your body in motion than to restart it from rest. Your flutter kick helps maintain flow and ease, both of which are critical to successful, effective drill practice.

For those whose ankles are so rigid that legs-only forward motion is virtually hopeless, we recommend using Slim Fins, which we have found to be the most effective in providing an effortless, natural flutter. For those with just enough ankle mobility that there is some chance of a moderate, not-too-tiring flutter, we usually find that they simply have to unlearn bad habits.

The most common bad habit is kicking from the knees, rather than from the hips. When your ankles won't flex, something else has to flex in flutter kicking. That something else is almost always the knee. Before long your knee-flexing, quadriceps-tiring kick (like running or pedaling) is laying down muscle memory for an ineffective kick. We have found VK to be the best quick fix. VK is better than prone or even side kicking for training your legs to move efficiently because it removes the influence of gravity, which often causes people to bend their legs too much when kicking on a board. VK also works because it leaves you no choice but to flutter efficiently. You can't do what I describe on the following pages without an efficient flutter. Within a few minutes you understand how that action should feel, and what muscles are working when you do it right. Once you understand that, it's much easier to keep kicking the right way while drilling.

For that reason, while you are engaged in mastering Lesson One, it's a good idea to do some VK in the warmup and at regular intervals throughout your drill practice sessions. Here are the basics:

1. Stay as vertical and as "tall" as possible with the longest possible line from the top of your head to your toes. Feel as if you're "sky-hooked" by a line at the top of your head. Avoid bending at the waist or leaning either forward or back.
2. If you've never practiced this before, cross your arms over your chest or even tuck a pull buoy under each armpit.

Cross your arms over your chest for the best vertical-kicking position.

Your chin should be in the water with your mouth barely above the surface. Or your mouth may be just below the surface; if so, lean your head back slightly when you need a breath.

When working on the flutter kick, move your legs as a pendulum. Kick from the top of your leg, not from the knee. Rather than trying to rigidly point your toes, simply focus on a long leg line from hip to toes. A *supple* leg will bend just as much as needed.

Kick from the top of your leg, not from the knee, and keep the kick within the "shadow" of your body.

The most efficient kick is the one that uses the least effort. Keep your kick fairly compact, as if within the body's "shadow." Aim for a feeling of light and steady fluttering with a sense of stillness and stability in your body position. A larger kick will feel labored.

Kick with equal emphasis both forward and back. Maintain intensity and tempo steady enough to hold your mouth just above the surface.

When you first practice VK, alternate 15 seconds of kicking with 15 seconds of rest (holding on to the wall or lane line, or treading water, or floating on your back). The object of this practice is to learn to hold a stable, aligned, vertical position with your chin right at the surface with the least possible energy expenditure.

As you improve at VK, begin applying what you learn to your drilling. You can do this in two ways. One is to start with 10 to 15 seconds of kicking in deep water, then, while keeping your kick steady, gradually lie back into a balanced supine position (Drill #1.1) and move down the pool. A second suggestion is to do a series of 50-yard repeats, starting from the deep end. Kick vertically for 10 to 15 seconds, then rest briefly and do one of your Lesson One drills for 25 yards, moving your legs exactly as you did while vertical, but with the lightest effort. Rest briefly before doing another 25 yards of the same drill or another Lesson One drill with heightened awareness of how you use your kick. Don't **try** to kick more. Just feel what happens naturally as a result of going vertical first.

Besides using VK to drill more efficiently, you can also use it purely as a kicking exercise – one far more valuable than kicking on a board. You can vary the intensity of the exercise in two ways – moving your arms higher or doing "fartlek" sets (alternating easy and hard). The best kickers may be able to briefly keep the head above water even with the arms extended overhead. Some coaches ask their swimmers to hold light weights (3 to 5 pounds) overhead while kicking. For a "fartlek" training set, kick with arms higher for 10 to 30 seconds, then lower them for a similar period.

And please remember: The greatest initial value of VK is not to help you kick faster. It's to allow you to maintain flow and momentum during drills while putting the *least* energy into your kick.

Lesson Two: Dynamic Balance

Each of the drills in Lesson One helps you become balanced (effortlessly horizontal) in a static position. The drills in Lesson Two will help you learn how to maintain equilibrium while moving among the positions mastered in Lesson One. This is called dynamic balance, and it's how you'll balance while swimming.

We'll continue using head-lead drills (arms at your sides) to cultivate the skill of using weight shifts, rather than your arms, to initiate rotation. These drills will also introduce long-axis rotation. We'll begin with very simple and basic LA rotation and gradually increase the skill level. The final drill will include LA rotation skills of a higher order than you'll need even while swimming.

Drill #2.1: Active Side Balance: Nose Up/Nose Down

Why do this drill: The Sweet Spot is the position in which you'll start and finish all long-axis drills, but the 90-degree position in which we practice side balance in Lesson One, Drill #1.3 is also critical and integral to all freestyle drills. There will be a pause in that position before rolling – or switching – to the other side. During that pause, you'll check your new position to ensure you're still on your side. You'll also use that moment to mentally rehearse what comes next. In order to do all the freestyle drills well, it's essential to be able to move easily from Sweet Spot to 90 degrees and back again. For freestylers, this is also one of the two best positions for kicking sets.

Follow this sequence:

1. Start by balancing in your Sweet Spot. Stay there, kicking gently, until you feel balanced and aligned...

2.   ... then swivel your head to look at the bottom, rolling to 90 degrees as you do. While looking down, check to see if your "dry" hip and shoulder are pointing straight up. Also check if your head is hidden and your arm is dry from shoulder to wrist.

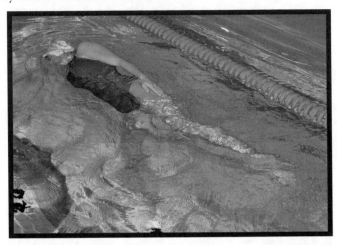

3.   After a while (remain nose-down for as long as you feel comfortable, without *trying* to hold your breath), return to your Sweet Spot by swiveling your head to look up and rolling your body back to where you started. Take at least three "cleansing breaths" before you swivel/roll to the nose-down position again.

4.   Practice on both sides until you can move easily back and forth between the two positions with economy and subtlety. While nose down, you should feel a more pronounced sense of going "downhill."

5.   In both positions, continue to focus on your sense of slipping a long, clean bodyline through the smallest possible hole in the water.

Advance to the next drill when: You have a strong awareness of when you are in Sweet Spot and when you are at 90 degrees and can move smoothly between the two. *Caution:* Advancing to the next drill definitely does not mean putting this one behind you. This is one of the best warmup drills for a long-axis skill practice because it puts you in touch with the two key positions that launch every freestyle drill. It is also one of the most valuable ways to practice flutter kicking, teaching far more than prone kicking with a kickboard.

Drill #2.2: Active Balance: Looking Up

Why do this drill: This is one more way to practice the skill of maintaining equilibrium while moving smartly among balance positions. It also introduces the exact form of active balance you will use when swimming backstroke and allows you to practice the stable-head/rolling-body that is critical to fluent backstroke.

Follow this sequence:

1. Start by balancing in your Sweet Spot. Stay there, kicking gently, until you are sure of your balance and alignment.

2. Keeping your head perfectly steady, roll smoothly to your other Sweet Spot. Stay there until you feel balanced and stable, before rolling back to your starting point.

3. Continue practicing economical rotation from one side to the other. As you practice, your goals are to improve your stability and stillness this way:
4. Keep your head hidden and fixed at all times. To reinforce this, imagine you're carrying a cup of water on your head and avoid spilling a drop as you roll from side to side. (We sometimes have swimmers practice this while balancing a half-filled water bottle on the forehead, until they can easily do a full length without losing it.)
5. While in your Sweet Spot, imagine you're carrying a cup of water on your "dry" shoulder without spilling a drop. Hold this image until you have a sense of *stillness* in your practice.

Continue practicing this drill until: You feel stable and supported at all times and consistently hit your Sweet Spot in good balance, with a dry arm and hand at the moment you finish rolling. You can roll from Sweet Spot to Sweet Spot with the least possible turbulence and wake. You can roll from side to side, purely using weight shifts without using your hands to help.

Drill #2.3: Active Balance: Looking Down

Why do this drill: This drill provides a sterner test of your balance skills and coordination. It also introduces and develops two new skills that will be critical to all of the freestyle drills that follow: *Rolling your body like a log* and leading rotation from the core, not from your head.

Follow this sequence:
1. Start by balancing in your Sweet Spot. Stay there, kicking gently, until you are sure of your balance and alignment.

2. Swivel your head to the nose-down position. Pause to check that you are
    well balanced at exactly 90 degrees.

3. Roll your body — like a log — to your Sweet Spot on the other side. This
    means move everything — head, shoulders, torso, hips — as a unit and
    stay balanced and horizontal as you do.

4. Take three deep, slow, *cleansing* breaths and be sure you are rebalanced in your Sweet Spot before repeating the sequence back to where you started.

5. Do each rotation as if you were trying to take your bellybutton to the air. This will form a habit of rolling from the core, not leading rotation with your head, and make it more likely that you'll roll all the way to your Sweet Spot. Your objective is to have your bodyroll take your mouth to where the air is. Your head simply "goes along for the ride" as your body rolls.

Continue practicing this drill until: You roll your body as a coordinated, integrated unit and consistently finish each rotation right in your Sweet Spot. It takes only a moment to rebalance and regain your equilibrium after each rotation.

Drill #2.4: Active Balance: Full Circle

Why do this drill: This drill is the most advanced test of active long-axis balance. It combines the two previous drills to heighten your sense of alignment, control, and coordination by moving through a full 360-degree rotation. This is also the first drill to link the common skills of backstroke and freestyle in a single drill, improving your "fluency foundation" for each stroke more than is possible with single-stroke drills.

Follow this sequence:

1. Start by balancing in your Sweet Spot as in each of the previous three drills.

2.   Swivel your head and look directly down. Pause to check your 90-degree balance (head hidden, arm showing).

3.   Roll your body like a log to your Sweet Spot on the other side. Pause and rebalance. Keep your head steady – looking up – and, as in Drill #2.2 above, rotate back to your original Sweet Spot. Pause and rebalance, then repeat. Practice rolling in both directions, staying balanced at all times.

   Continue practicing this drill until: You can roll smoothly like a log while doing the freestyle-oriented (looking down while rolling) part of this drill and can keep your head hidden and fixed while doing the backstroke-oriented (looking up while rolling) part of this drill. Maintaining your alignment becomes much more challenging while moving through the full circle in this drill. To help, imagine you have a laser beam connecting the top of your head and one point on the far wall ahead of you at every moment.

Practice Tips for Lesson Two

   This completes Lesson Two – Active Balance. As with Lesson One practice, once you have learned the basic mechanics for each drill, you should work patiently and persistently at Lesson Two skills until all struggle, unease, and discomfort are a thing of the past. While Lesson Two drills are more challenging than those in Lesson One, the movements are still much simpler than whole-stroke swimming. Such drills are your *best* opportunity to replace habits of inefficiency and struggle with flow, ease, comfort, and control. You can make that transformation more enduring if you continue practicing with the least possible effort and mainly in repeats of 25 yards or less.

Once you've learned the basic coordination and sequencing, turn your focus to the *qualities* of fluent drilling. Your goal is to consistently do all these drills with virtually no turbulence or wake, with the lightest possible kick, to feel as if you're slipping your body through a very small hole in the water. And to consistently trigger each rotation with weight shifts in your core and a feeling that your head just goes along for the ride. Also continue to minimize the importance of how many or how fast. The pace clock can't tell you anything of value during this phase of stroke development.

Lesson Three:
Learn Slippery Long-Axis Body Positions

We'll switch from head-lead drills to hand-lead drills in this lesson. If you have faithfully followed the prescriptions in the two previous lessons, you should now be able to creatively use the water to carry you by proper head positioning and weight distribution. The hand-lead drills in this lesson will provide two important insights: how you will experience balance while swimming (because your weight distribution is different with an arm extended than with both arms at your sides) and how to make yourself maximally slippery in the long-axis strokes. In this lesson, we also begin to "set up" the freestyle-specific drills of Lesson 4.

Drill #3.1: Hand-Lead Sweet Spot —
Lengthen Your "Vessel"

Why do this drill: Mastering this position will let you move smoothly to all freestyle and backstroke drills. It teaches you how balance will feel with an arm extended, and imprints your most slippery drilling position. It also establishes the exact position in which you'll start and finish every subsequent long-axis drill. In Lesson One, Drill #1.3, you've already found your best side-balance position — your Sweet Spot. When you extend your arm, nothing changes; your Hand-Lead Sweet Spot will be exactly the same as your Head-Lead Sweet Spot.

Follow this sequence:

1. Balance in your Sweet Spot, with both arms at your sides. Are you hiding your head? Are you showing your arm? If so, then...

2. ... "sneak" your lower arm to full extension. When fully outstretched, your hand should be a couple of inches below the surface. Your palm can be up, down, or sideways.

3. Check the gap between the *back* of your head and your "wet" shoulder. Narrow that gap to the extent possible, but avoid strain or discomfort.

4. Next, check to make sure you're still "hiding" your head and "showing" your other arm.

    Continue practicing this drill until: You feel as if you could glide blissfully in this position on either side all day long. (When we teach this drill at workshops, we emphasize the importance of ease and comfort by telling our students that we'll keep teaching "until we see BLISS on your faces.") Be sensitive also for evidence of tension or strain, such as craning the neck, arching the back, or sculling the lower hand. You should also feel like a long, balanced needle, slipping through the smallest possible hole in the water. When you feel this, it should take remarkably little kicking effort to cross the pool. Keep practicing until this describes you.

Drill #3.2: Kick in the Skating Position

Why do this drill: We follow precisely the same skill progression as we did in the head-lead drill sequence. First learn Sweet Spot, then make it active. That's what we do here, but now in a hand-lead position. This movement sequence – moving smoothly from nose up in Sweet Spot to nose down at 90 degrees — will start all subsequent freestyle drills. This is also the *second* of the two best positions for freestyle kicking sets. (Hand-Lead Sweet Spot was the first.)

Follow this sequence:

1. Start in your Sweet Spot exactly as in Drill #3.1, with arm extended. Kick there gently, until you feel balanced and aligned...

2. ... then swivel your head to look at the bottom, rolling to 90 degrees as you do. While looking down, check to see if your body is at 90 degrees with your "dry" hip and shoulder pointing straight up. Check to see if your head is hidden and your arm is exposed from shoulder to wrist. Your extended hand should be several inches below the surface and palm-down.

3. In this position, you should feel a heightened sense of support and of going downhill.
4. After a comfortable interval (don't test how long you can hold your breath), return to your Sweet Spot by looking up again as you roll back to where you started. Turn your hand palm up again, if that's more comfortable.
5. Take at least three "cleansing breaths" before you swivel/roll to the nose-down/90-degree position again.
6. Practice on both sides until you can move smoothly back and forth between the two positions. Continue to focus on slipping a long, clean bodyline through the smallest possible hole in the water, in both positions.

Continue practicing this drill until: You maintain perfect balance and ease as your body rotates effortlessly between Sweet Spot and 90 degrees. The critical skill you should be committing to muscle memory in this drill is to get *all the way back to your Sweet Spot* when you look up again. If you take the time necessary to make this movement feel natural in this drill – when you don't have much else to think about – you'll be much better prepared to continue doing it when you progress to the freestyle "Switch" drills.

Drill #3.3: Shark Fin

Why do this drill: I think of this drill as something of a sidebar. It doesn't fit quite as seamlessly into the movement sequence but it is quite useful, at this point, as a balance test. If you can do this drill easily, you should be able to breeze through all the other freestyle drills with impeccable balance. If not, you'll need to keep a primary focus on balance, going downhill, keeping your weight shifted forward, etc.

Shark Fin also begins to establish the pattern for a more compact and efficient recovery. It greatly exaggerates the recovery style we wish to end up with, but in doing so makes it easier to examine and modify what you're doing now.

Follow this sequence:

1. Balance in your Hand-Lead Sweet Spot, then swivel your head and look directly down, just as in the previous drill. Pause to check that you are right at 90 degrees and that you feel well supported by the water.

2. Slide your hand up your side. Do this with your elbow leading and your hand trailing, thumb dragging along your ribs, as if you were pulling up a zipper from waist to armpit.

3. How does this affect your balance? Can you glide along serenely with your elbow pointing skyward above your shoulder and little change in your body position? If so, great. Stay there for a while. You'll learn more about how weight distribution affects balance. After a while, slide it back down, look up again, and rebalance *in your Sweet Spot.* Then repeat the sequence. Keep every movement separate and distinct. Don't rush.

4. If you feel yourself start to sink as soon as you begin to slide your hand upward, then just bring it to your shoulder and immediately slide it back down. In either case, continue to reinforce the habit of returning to Sweet Spot and relaxing there until you feel in control before doing another cycle of the drill.

Continue practicing this drill until: You can sense how stable and supported you are as your arm slides to the Shark Fin position. Practice on both sides. Stay relaxed; eliminate all tension from your recovering arm. Take at least 3 *cleansing breaths* after returning to Sweet Spot, before you swivel/roll to look down again.

Drill #3.4: Easy-Anchors Freestyle
(Not on Long-Axis Video)

Why do this drill: In workshops, I'm only half joking when I say, "We give you this drill to make the next one feel easy." This does require patience and persistence to reach the point of feeling you do it well. But once you've mastered it, you'll have learned a LOT about how to maintain control and equilibrium while rolling from one side to the other. It's also extremely valuable because it introduces you to the critical skill of *anchoring your hand* to hold on to your place in the water as your body moves by.

Follow this sequence:

1. Start in Head-Lead Sweet Spot (back to head-lead for this drill).
2. Once balanced, sneak your hand to full extension.

3. When you feel stable and comfortable, roll/swivel to the nose-down/90-degree position. Pause to check that you're looking directly at the bottom, that you're balanced, and that you feel as if you're "going downhill."

4. Anchor your hand. Do this by flexing your wrist to point your fingertips
    toward the bottom and rotating your elbow up or forward slightly until
    your entire arm feels like a "big paddle."

5. After anchoring your hand, just hold on to the water with that hand as
    you roll to your Sweet Spot on the other side. Your trailing arm doesn't
    move; it stays right on your side.

6. After rolling, you'll be back in Head-Lead Sweet Spot on the other side. Take 3 cleansing breaths and all the time you need to feel balanced and relaxed, before sneaking your arm up, swiveling to nose-down/90 degrees, and repeating the drill in the other direction.

Keep practicing this drill until: You have a sense of being connected and controlled as you roll from one side to the other. Here are the points that will get you there. (*These will all be critical skills to every freestyle Switch drill in Lesson Four.* If you can master them here, they'll be *much* easier to execute in the Switch drills.)

1. After you look down, roll as if you are going to *breathe with your bellybutton.* This will help you initiate the movement from your core, rather than leading with your head. It will also make it more likely that you'll finish your rotation in good balance and in your Sweet Spot.

2. Maintain a focus on moving your head, arm, and torso as a unit. Avoid having a sense of *pulling* your hand back. Strive to maintain a feeling of keeping your hand and arm connected to your torso and holding on to a spot in the water as you roll.

Lesson Four: Freestyle "Switch" Drills

This lesson brings together all of the skills and movements mastered thus far and, in a quick and simple sequence, teaches the movements of a fluent freestyle stroke. Your dynamic balance, coordinated and integrated core-centered rotation, slippery body positions, and understanding of how to link the propelling armstroke to core-body rotation have all prepared you to swim a Fishlike Freestyle. This 4-step sequence will make it happen. It also introduces you to the effortless propulsion that can result when you connect your propelling armstroke to the full power of the kinetic chain.

Drill #4.1: Under Switch (Not on Long-Axis Video)

Why do this drill: This is the first drill in which we tap the full potential of the kinetic chain. This fantastic and nearly effortless source of propulsive power is wasted unless you link your armstroke to core-body rotation. We introduce that linkage in a simple way in this drill by giving you a visual cue for when to make the switch.

Follow this sequence:

1. Start in Hand-Lead Sweet Spot. After you feel balanced and stable, look down and pause. Be sure you are balanced at 90 degrees.

2. Sneak your "dry" arm forward under the water, with your hand sliding across your chest and under your jaw.

3. *When you can see your hand in front of your face,* switch and roll to your Sweet Spot on the other side, extending that arm forward as you do.

4. Take three deep, cleansing breaths as you check your position and balance to make sure you're in your Hand-Lead Sweet Spot again. Whenever you feel ready, repeat in the other direction.

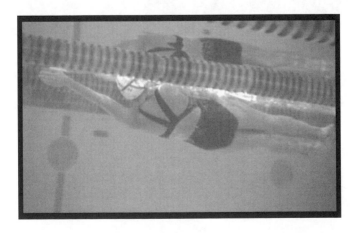

Continue to practice this drill until: Each move is smooth and controlled, and, when you roll, you move everything as a unit. We put extra emphasis on leading with your bellybutton and rolling like a log in previous drills because we want those motions to come naturally in this drill series. It is also just as important as previously to maintain your focus on *moving your body through the smallest possible "hole" in the water* and on doing the drill as silently as possible. Last, but not least, always wait until you see your recovering hand right under your nose before switching. This is the only time you'll have a visual cue for that and it's an invaluable opportunity to teach yourself "switch timing."

Drill #4.2: "Zipper" Switch

Before doing this drill for the first time, review Drill #3.3, Shark Fin, for five minutes; it will be valuable preparation for the main skill taught here.

Why do this drill: It teaches and imprints a compact, economical, and highly efficient recovery. On the Under Switch, you recover your arm under water, leading with your fingertips. In actual swimming, your elbow leads. We'll begin practicing that here, but with a partially submerged recovery; the confinement and drag you experience on hand and forearm help to make you more aware of how you recover and where you re-enter the water. This drill will have you do both in an exaggerated way. Once we reduce focus on those points in the next drill, that exaggeration should help you continue to do things right. Because you will lose the visual cue for when to make the switch, you'll have to use kinesthetic awareness for timing your switch.

Follow this sequence:

1.   Start exactly as in Under Switch, but after you look down and pause...

2.   ... drag the trailing hand and forearm through the water (with elbow held high) until the hand comes alongside your ear...

3. ... then slice the arm forward to full extension as you switch and roll to your Sweet Spot on the other side. The recovery action should be initiated as in Shark Fin. Lead with the elbow and drag your hand along your side (but under water) as if pulling a zipper up your side. Your body remains at 90 degrees the entire time you "pull up the zipper."

4. Feel the drag and confinement of the water against your hand and wrist. Use that feeling to keep the recovery compact. Don't fight the drag. Minimize it by keeping your hand relaxed.

5. When you sense that your hand is next to your ear, slice it down and forward as if putting your arm into the sleeve of a jacket. This action triggers your "switch" or roll to your Sweet Spot on the other side.

6. Relax and glide there for as long as you want (I suggest using 3 cleansing breaths as a regulator of your pacing), then repeat in the other direction.

    Continue to practice this drill until: A compact, efficient recovery begins to feel natural and you know exactly the right moment to switch and link your armstroke to the action of the kinetic chain. As these drills become progressively more dynamic – tapping more of the momentum created by having all of your body mass roll as a unit – you should feel more acceleration with no more effort. One camper described this sensation as feeling yourself "squirt forward."

Drill #4.3: Over Switch
(Formerly Called Stop-Stop Switch)

Why do this drill: It helps you swim tall and with effortless power by connecting your balanced, rotating core body with your propelling armstroke while teaching FQS stroke timing. After using a visual cue to imprint timing in Under Switch and using exaggeration to imprint a compact recovery in Zipper Switch, we will now begin using the more natural recovery of swimming. We will retain one element of exaggeration here — having the hand enter right next to the goggles to correct a tendency common among most swimmers to over-reach on the entry.

Follow this sequence:

1. Start exactly as in the previous two drills, but after you look down and pause...

2.   ... bring your "dry" arm forward with normal-but-compact recovery.

3.   *Swipe your thumb* along the side of your head, right next to your goggles.

4. Slice your hand into the water *right next to your goggles*, then extend it forward with the same arm-into-sleeve sensation emphasized in Zipper Switch.

5. That swipe-and-slice action also triggers the switch-and-roll that takes you to your Sweet Spot on the other side. Once there, relax and glide (3 cleansing breaths) before repeating in the other direction.

Continue to practice this drill until: All the habits cultivated on the previous two drills feel completely natural on this one: Roll like a log; lead with your core; slip your hand and arm through a "sleeve" in the water. In fact, add another image here: *Your rotating body should follow your arm down the sleeve.* Take all the time you need to feel "in your bones" the right moment in your recovery to make the switch and trigger the kinetic chain. Once you do, you can leave out the thumb-swipe.

Drill #4.4: Triple Switch

Why do this drill: This drill gives you a seamless transition from freestyle drilling to freestyle swimming. You'll actually *be* swimming during most of this drill, but will still have time for evaluation and adjustment when you go back to Sweet Spot. This drill is also ideal for refining your timing and rhythm and learning to use core-based weight shifts as the new rhythm-source for swimming.

Follow this sequence:

1. Balance in your Hand-Lead Sweet Spot, then swivel to 90 degrees and look directly down (same as in the three previous drills), and pause there for one count before you...

2. ... do three consecutive "switches" without breathing and without inter-
    ruption, before rolling to your Sweet Spot on the other side.

3. Once there, relax, glide, and rebalance (3 cleansing breaths) before re-
    peating in the other direction.
4. During the three switches, keep looking directly at the bottom and keep
    your head "hidden" and absolutely still.

5. Practice *triple* versions of all three types of "Switch" drills (Under, Zipper, and Over). Triple Under may be your most valuable drill for learning easy balance and leisurely, rhythmic, core-based swimming.

Continue to practice this drill until: Your recovery, hand entry, and the timing of your switches become consistent, unhurried, and rhythmic. During the three switches you have the opportunity to practice several skills that are critical to carry over into swimming. These include:

- Keep your head hidden and stable. Some swimmers have a tendency to wag or turn the head during the three switches. At workshops I instruct swimmers to keep watching the tiles on the dark line on the pool bottom slide past them as they do the switches.
- Keep your switches unhurried. Another common tendency is to slip back into old habits of just churning the arms because this drill feels a lot like swimming. Keep your rhythm slow and patient. Wait for the recovery arm to pass your ear before making the switch.
- Develop your sense that it's body-rhythm that governs your stroke. Initially, you'll focus on how the arms time your switches, but you should gradually shift to feeling your switches as rhythmic weight shifts. As that sense emerges, tune into it and let it take over most of your consciousness. This is how you will learn to swim with your body.
- Once you feel body rhythms emerging, adjust your degree of body roll to allow for the most fluid and rhythmic movement.

Drill #4.5: Single-Arm Freestyle: The Total Immersion Way

This drill is not an integral part of our learning sequence, but mastering it as a supplement to the essential drills *will* make you a much better freestyler. Moreover, Single-Arm (or "right arm, left arm") is probably the most popular of all freestyle drills. Yet as most people do it, it's a poorly designed drill: You start in a flat, prone position, both arms extended and streamlined, pull one arm, rolling to breathe as you do, then return to the flat-with-arms-extended position. The main point of the drill is to examine and work on each part of the armstroke – catch, insweep, outsweep, thumb brushing hip, etc. In other words, it's a classic "Human Swimming" drill mostly focused on "how you push water toward your feet." Our version puts the focus on your core body.

The first change is that you start and finish this drill in your Sweet Spot, rather than flat on your stomach. Second: with each arm cycle you roll completely to both sides, as you do in swimming, rather than a half-roll to the side you're stroking on. Third: you propel by anchoring your hand and using body rotation to move your body past it, rather than by pushing water toward your feet. And, finally, since you are "challenged" in your balance by having the non-stroking arm at your side and breathing toward the "unsupported" side, you are forced to "find your center" — or balance — in your body's core.

Once you've learned the basics and gotten comfortable with this drill, raise your learning curve again by practicing it with fistgloves to improve your hand-anchoring skills.

What to focus on:

Start in your Sweet Spot. On your right side, bottom arm extended. Is your head hidden? Are you "showing" your left arm, as it lies on your side?

Look down. Swivel your head and look directly at the bottom, head in line with your spine. Pause for one count to make sure you're still hiding your head and showing your right arm. You should still be effortlessly balanced.

"Anchor" your hand. Think of your right hand and forearm as one big paddle. Use them to hold on to your place in the water, as if there was a handle you could grab to pull yourself past it. Rotate your elbow slightly above your hand to link it with the powerful muscles of your upper back.

Propel with body roll. As you hold on to the water, simply roll your left hip down to move your body past your hand's anchoring point. Keep looking down as you do.

Roll like a log. Keep your head and spine aligned and move your arm-head-torso as a unit as you roll your body like a log

See your hand again. Keep looking down until you see your right hand re-enter the water. Cut a "hole" in the water with your fingertips and slide your arm into that hole (as if putting your arm in a sleeve). Do this without making a splash or disturbing the water.

Lengthen your body. As your right shoulder enters the water it pushes your fingertips forward to make your "vessel" long and sleek. Your arm should be weightless with no downward pressure on it.

Roll back to your Sweet Spot. Finish exactly where you started. Stay there, kicking gently in effortless balance, until your breathing normalizes, then start the next cycle as above. Switch sides on the next length.

Practice Tips for Lesson Four

The drills in this lesson will, over the long term, become your most-used freestyle drills so it's essential that you give yourself plenty of time to become thoroughly acquainted with and completely masterful at them. While practicing the first three Switch drills, put your greatest focus on switching as a unit, leading from the core, sliding your arm down the sleeve, and slipping your body through that sleeve as well. The focus point that seems to pull every element neatly together is doing these drills as silently as possible.

Lesson Five: Backstroke Drills
Before You Begin

When we begin teaching balance on the back, which will later translate into balanced backstroke swimming, we start by teaching how to hide your head. When on your back this means we want to see just the face, and nothing more, visible above the surface. And the face should be exactly parallel to the surface.

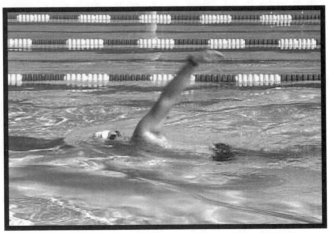

"Hiding your head" in backstrokes means having just your face visible above the surface.

Two of the most common errors are to have the chin jutting toward the ceiling or to have it tucked into the throat. It's truly striking how you will become instantly better balanced as soon as you get your head and neck aligned (just get into the position you'd be in if standing erect) and hide your head (press in enough at the back of your head and top of your spine so that just your face shows above the surface). Among all elite swimmers today, Lenny Krayzelburg is the best example of the head position that allows you to bal-

ance and swim with far more ease. The idea with balance is *not* to work at it; it's to make it effortless, and the starting point is to get head position right.

One more note about backstroke drills. Because backstroke is so completely a finesse-and-feel stroke (not much power is available when you're on your back), we've found that fistgloves have even more magical effect in these drills than in others.

Drill # 5.1: Active Balance: Nose Up (Review)

Why do this drill: We introduced this drill in Lesson Two. It is the perfect intro to backstroke skills so you should review it now, before continuing through the backstroke lesson. It will help imprint the stable-head/rolling-body movement that is at the heart of all the drills that follow and is critical to fluent backstroke.

Reminders:

1. Kick gently in your Sweet Spot. Stay there for 3 deep, slow breaths, until you feel like an effortlessly balanced arrow. Then...

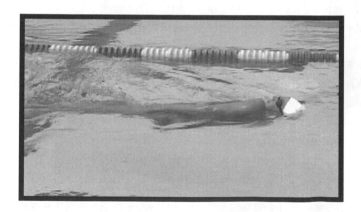

2. ... keeping your head steady (imagine carrying a champagne glass on your forehead), roll smoothly to your other Sweet Spot.

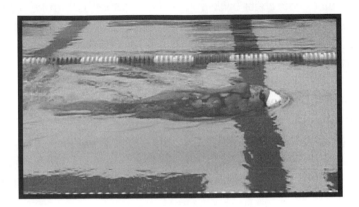

3. Continue practicing economical rotation from one side to the other, until you feel stability and stillness even as you roll.
4. As you roll, lean steadily on your upper back, until your hips feel light. You should also feel a dry patch of thigh on each rotation.
5. Also focus on rolling from side to side without using your hands to help.

Drill # 5.2: Easy-Anchors Backstroke

Why do this drill: Learn how to link a propelling armstroke to the active balance you practiced in the previous drill. It will reinforce your sense of maintaining perfect equilibrium and stability while employing full body roll.

Follow this sequence:

1. Start by balancing in your Sweet Spot. Stay there for 3 deep, slow breaths, kicking gently, until you feel balance and alignment. Then...

2. ... *sneak* your bottom (underwater) arm over your head and anchor your hand. Pause a moment. Then...

3. Hold onto the water as you roll smoothly to your other Sweet Spot. Stay
    there for 3 deep, slow breaths, perfectly balanced and stable, before *sneak-*
    ing your other arm overhead to begin the next cycle.

Drill #5.3: Slide-and-Glide Backstroke

Why do this drill: Links the recovery arm to the propelling arm in the
backstroke body roll taught by the two previous drills.

Follow this sequence:

1. Start by balancing for 3 deep, slow breaths in your Sweet-Spot needle
    shape with one arm extended. Then...

2. Stroke with your leading arm while recovering your trailing arm, and roll directly to your Sweet Spot on the other side. Stay there for 3 deep, slow breaths in perfect balance, then roll back again.

3. Keep your head hidden and fixed at all times. Imagine you're carrying a champagne glass on your forehead and avoid spilling a drop as you roll from needle shape to needle shape. (Or actually practice this while balancing a half-filled water bottle on your forehead, until you can do a full length without dropping the bottle.)

4. Continue practicing until you can roll from side to side, hitting your Sweet-Spot needle shape immediately as you complete each rotation.

Drill # 5.4: Triple-Switch Backstroke
(Not illustrated on video, but simple to learn.)

Why do this drill: Provides a seamless transition from drilling to swimming while helping you retain great balance, alignment, and core-body rotation.

Follow this sequence:

1. Start by balancing for 3 deep, slow breaths in your Sweet-Spot needle shape with one arm extended.

2. Take three normal strokes (hand hits) of backstroke. As you finish the third stroke, roll to your Sweet Spot (dry arm and wrist, head hidden, needle shape) on the other side and stay long enough to be sure you are in perfect balance.

3. As you practice, particularly during the three strokes, focus on:

4. Keeping your head hidden and fixed – as if carrying a champagne glass.

5. Smooth, relaxed, rhythmic and needle-like core-body rotation.

6. Making your stroke feel as much like the drills as possible.

Drill #5.5: Single-Arm Backstroke

Why do this drill: This continues to reinforce your balanced, aligned, needle shape, and links it to your propelling armstroke, while putting a bit more emphasis on rolling fully to both sides on every stroke.

Follow this sequence:

1. Start by balancing for 3 deep, slow breaths in your Sweet-Spot needle shape with one arm extended.

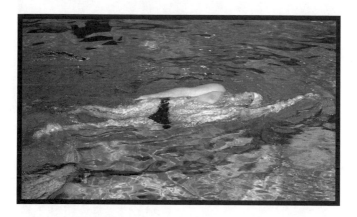

2. Stroke with the leading arm only, rolling so that the shoulder of the leading (stroking) arm rolls clear of the water.

3.   Reach for the sky on the recovery.

4.   As the recovering hand enters the water, roll the shoulder of the trailing arm clear of the water. Pause for a moment in Hand-Lead Sweet Spot before starting the next cycle. Switch arms each length.

Drill #5.6: Alternating Single-Arm Backstroke

Why do this drill: It imprints continuous and fluid arm action and body roll. It also provides an additional seamless transition from drilling to whole-stroke backstroke.

Follow this sequence:

1.   Start by balancing for 3 deep, slow breaths in your Sweet-Spot needle shape with one arm extended.
2.   Take 2 strokes of backstroke with your leading arm, then 2 strokes with the other arm, continuing to emphasize rolling **each** shoulder clear of the water on **every** cycle.
3.   Keep the arm action continuous and fluid.

4. The arm-exchange cycle, in which you take the second stroke with one arm, followed by the first with the other, will introduce how whole-stroke swimming should feel. Refer to the video for a strong visual aid.

Apply the Lessons: Swim Backstroke

It is an excellent learning aid to swim a little bit (five to ten minutes) of whole-stroke backstroke after each drill, before progressing to the next drill. This will work best if you alternate a length of the drill you have just practiced with a length of swimming. In each, simply try to let your whole-stroke back-stroke feel as much like the drill as possible, perhaps sensing that sameness become a bit stronger with each repeat. When swimming, keep it simple. Focus mainly on:

- Keeping your head hidden and fixed (as if carrying a water bottle on your forehead)
- Leaning on your upper back (shifting the pressure from one side to another as you roll)
- Feeling that your hips are light, and showing a dry patch of thigh on each stroke.
- Developing your rhythm from the core, not from your arms.

Lesson Six: Long-Axis Combination Drills

Long-Axis Combination (LA Combo) drills combine free and back, both drilling and swimming, to make each stroke even more fishlike than usually occurs when practicing the drills for either stroke, alone. In both strokes, these drills build a stronger instinct for slipping a long, sleek, vessel through a tiny "hole" in the water. And the rotation from free-to-back and back-to-free teaches you to slip through the water like an arrow through the air, using your core-body rotation more and more effectively to minimize drag and maximize effortless propulsion. The freestyle elements help your backstroke, while the backstroke elements help your freestyle.

Drill # 6.1: Sweet-Spot LA Combo

Why do this drill: This combines a freestyle foundation drill with a backstroke drill to heighten the fundamentals of balance, alignment, and rotation that make both strokes far more efficient. This drill provides an excellent way to practice and experience a heightened sense of sliding your body through a small hole in the water.

Follow this sequence:

1. Balance in Hand-Lead Sweet Spot.
2. Do one full cycle of Slide-and-Glide Backstroke, then look down...pause...and do one full cycle of Over Switch.
3. Take 3 deep, slow breaths and rebalance in your Sweet Spot before repeating the sequence.
4. Stay *tall*, as you switch from backstroke to freestyle and from free to back.
5. Slip your body through the smallest possible hole in the water at all times.

Drill #6.2: LA-Combo Swimming

Why do this drill: This is technically not a drill. It's really whole-stroke swimming done in a way that imprints effortless body rotation and intensifies your sense of being a long, slippery vessel on *both* strokes. Alternating cycles of freestyle with cycles of backstroke – which includes a full 360-degrees of rotation in each combo cycle – will heighten your sense of balance, alignment, and timing to a greater degree than when you swim freestyle or backstroke alone.

Follow this sequence:

1. You may find it helpful to practice a bit of Triple Switch (Drill #4.4) to groove your freestyle timing before doing this drill.

2. Start with 4 strokes of backstroke, then roll to 3 "switches" of freestyle, then roll again and take 4 more strokes of backstroke. (Feel free to modify the number of strokes in either style up or down to create different effects.)

3. Stay *tall and aligned* as you switch from backstroke to freestyle and free to back.

4. Maintain a strong sense of slipping your body through a small hole in the water, particularly as you switch from one stroke to the other.

5. Focus on making your sense of balance and long-axis rotation feel the same in both strokes.

Drill #6.3: LA-Combo Single Arm

Why do this drill: Combining several cycles of our special form of freestyle single-arm drill with several cycles of our backstroke single-arm drill can further imprint effortless rotation and stroke length in both strokes. This drill can also develop your sense of using your hand to hold on to your place in the water, and to link each armstroke to core-body rotation.

Follow this sequence:

1. While you are learning this drill, review Single-Arm Freestyle (Drill #4.5) and Single-Arm Backstroke (Drill #5.5) before practicing this one.

2. Balance in Hand-Lead Sweet Spot, then start with 2 cycles of Single-Arm Freestyle.

3. Pause for 3 breaths in your Sweet Spot, then take two cycles of Single-Arm Backstroke. After the 2nd cycle...pause...look down again, and resume Single-Arm Freestyle.

4. Continue alternating cycles of free and back, returning each time to your Sweet Spot.

5. Use your extended hand to stay *tall* as you transition from one stroke to the other.

6. As in all drills, try to maintain a long, sleek, slippery, balanced bodyline, and rotate that line cleanly down the pool.

Practice Tips for Lesson Six:

• As with other drills, take time to familiarize yourself with the basics. LA Combo drills require more coordination, so give yourself time to master the basics. Remember, as with all drills, LA Combo drills provide a much more beneficial learning experience when done 100% right, than when done 99% right.

- Use our video *FREESTYLE AND BACKSTROKE: The Total Immersion Way* to get the most graphic sense of how these drills should be done; particularly with LA Combo drills, words on paper cannot convey their unusual beauty and grace.
- Especially in your first experiments with these drills, you'll be much more successful in achieving the right "feel" (kinesthetic awareness) if you practice the individual freestyle and backstroke elements first.
- Once they become no-brainers, try using these drills in the way I enjoy them most: longish (200 to 400 yards), relaxed (almost meditative) continuous swims in which I alternate 25 yards of an LA Combo drill, 25 yards of backstroke, 25 drill again, and 25 freestyle. It makes both strokes feel increasingly relaxed, smooth, and fluent.

Chapter 13

Short-Axis Drill Progressions

Lesson Seven: Short-Axis Balance and Rotation Drills

As I wrote earlier, balance in the long-axis strokes is constant, but dynamic. It's critically important to remain almost perfectly horizontal at all times, even as you roll rhythmically from side to side — almost a high-wire balance act for many novices. Balance in the short-axis strokes of butterfly and breaststroke is different. In fly and breast, you're *supposed* to give up your balance in every stroke cycle as you stroke, breathe, and recover. But you also need to rhythmically *rebalance* almost immediately to return your body to a slippery, horizontal — indeed a bit downhill — position as it is driven forward by the power and propulsion produced by the core-body rocking action. Rock upward to harness power and generate propulsion. Rock immediately back downward to maximize the distance you travel on that stroke. And, finally, you must do it all with minimum effort and maximum efficiency.

The secret is to use your torso muscles to do as much of the work as possible. Most swimmers rely too much on the arms and legs for power and propulsion. Those muscles get tired much more quickly, wasting the fitness developed through training. Core muscle is more resistant to fatigue, and can do most of the work far more efficiently. So we start the short-axis skill-building sequence with drills that teach you to move the body down the pool, using core-body rotation almost exclusively. The patterns and rhythms of these drills will later give your arms and legs their "marching orders."

The second key skill taught in this lesson is how to use your head to channel energy. In breast and fly, the body's fundamental movement is up and down. But the resulting travel must be *forward*. The head is the primary mechanism that determines how effectively you translate vertical energy into horizontal travel. In all three drills in this lesson you'll probably find it easier to keep the head close to a neutral position if you master the body movements described without breathing. Integrate the breathing only after you have mastered the body movements. Minimize the distraction of fitting in breathing by a) practicing initially for short distances and b) breathing only when necessary. Later you can include a regular breathing pattern.

Finally, I urge you, to make our video *BUTTERFLY AND BREASTSTROKE: The Total Immersion Way* part of your swimmer's tool bag. The movements described in this section are far too subtle to be described adequately by text or even illustrations. You will learn far more, far faster, by seeing them done on the video. The video also employs underwater, slow-motion, and freeze-frame to further enhance your learning.

Drill # 7.1 Head-Lead Body Dolphin

Why do this drill: Just as in freestyle and backstroke, we start our short-axis learning sequence with a head-lead drill, arms at your sides. Because you won't be able to use your arms for help of any sort, this drill will teach you to initiate the essential common movement of fly and breast in your core, rather than with your arms and legs. You'll also learn to use your head to lead your body through an undulating wave pattern. The point of undulating is to move forward – not to move up and down. Your head movements will channel the energy of undulation. Use your head to lead your body forward, while using your torso to provide the energy and power.

How to master short-axis skills faster: Fins can be a huge learning aid for those inexperienced in body dolphins. They amplify movement signals traveling from the core body to the toes. They put a "fish tail" on your human body, and this can be a great help in imitating a fishlike motion. Because fins help produce more forward flow, they give you clearer signals when you are doing things right. Finally, because they so greatly reduce the effort required, fins can help you stay relaxed and supple as you practice.

Follow this sequence:

1. Float in balance, face down, with arms at your sides, and start a relaxed rocking motion by rhythmically pressing your sternum and chest into the water... then...

... releasing your chest as shown below.

2. Each chest-press should barely submerge your head. Keep a "lazy chin," letting your nose pulse forward with each pulse.

3. Emphasize wave-***length***. With your head slipping just an inch or so below the surface, feel your forehead move toward the far end of the pool — rather than toward the bottom — with each pulse.

4. At first, focus only on making this movement supple, relaxed, and rhythmic, as shown on the video. Initially, practice for short distances, perhaps

6 or 8 pulses, until you feel your legs responding to your chest pulsing. Your body should begin to react to the pulsing the way a garden hose ripples when you shake it.

5. There is no overt kicking in the body dolphin; keep your thigh muscles relaxed. Keep your legs long and supple. Feel your bodyline — nose to toes — lengthen with each pulse. If you don't feel your body lengthen, try doing the drill with fins.

6. Breathe every 6 to 8 pulses at first. This will give you enough pulses to establish the body motion and rhythm. Breathing more often may interrupt your rhythm and flow.

7. When you breathe, do so without jutting your chin (feel almost as if you're wearing a neck brace).

8. Keep looking down and maintain your core-body pulsing rhythm through each breath. As you feel able to do this more seamlessly, you can gradually increase the frequency of your breathing. Eventually you can breathe every second or third pulse.

9.   When you are practicing for full pool lengths, you can measure your wave-length by counting how many pulses it takes to go 25 yards. With fins on, aim to finish a length in 20 or fewer pulses, with a relaxed flowing rhythm.

Advance to the next drill when: You can finish 25-yard lengths with little effort, no sense of breathlessness, with your legs remaining quite re-laxed, and in a fairly consistent number of pulses (in the teens if wearing fins.) You should also be able to do all this while breathing every 2nd or 3rd pulse. Take all the time necessary to reach this level of mastery; don't be in a hurry to push through the rest of the drills.

Drill # 7.2: Hand-Lead Body Dolphin

Why do this drill: It teaches you to use your hands to lengthen your bodyline and links the effortless and rhythmic body dolphin to a longer vessel.

Follow this sequence:

1.   Follow the same steps as in Drill #7.1 above with your arms extended forward, and with your hands shoulder width apart in order to relax your shoulders and to allow your torso to undulate freely. Keep your hands and wrists soft, so that they can gently undulate with your entire body.

2. Again emphasize wave-*length.* Each pulse should drive your fingertips toward the far end of the pool (not toward the bottom). Feel a slight stretch from fingers to toes each time you press in with your chest.

3. Release the pressure on your chest so that your body naturally rebounds back to the surface. Do not use your hands to push yourself back up, trusting the bouyancy of your lungs to bring your torso back to the surface. At this stage in the learning process, do this without taking a breath.

4. Though your hands are leading, continue to feel as if you're creating the wave with chest pulses. Your thigh muscles will be more involved, but avoid turning this into a kicking drill. Your feet should make no splash and should never leave the water. Fins can be very helpful in keeping your legs relaxed.

5. After you develop a natural rhythm, add a brief stretch-and-hold after every second or third pulse. Count the number of pulses you take per length and reduce the number it takes you to go 25 yards. With arms extended, your pulse-per-length count should improve by one or two over what it was in Head-Lead Body Dolphin.

6.   Breathe every 6 to 8 pulses at first. Gradually increase frequency until you
     are breathing every 2 to 3 pulses. Keep looking down and maintain your
     core-body pulsing rhythm through each breath.

Advance to the next drill when: You can finish 25-yard lengths with
little effort, no sense of breathlessness, with your legs remaining quite relaxed, and in a fairly consistent number of pulses (in the teens if wearing fins.)
You should also be able to do all this while breathing every 2nd or 3rd pulse.

Drill #7. 3: Find Your Corners

Why do this drill: This drill provides the most powerful link between essential core-body rotation and the breathing, rhythm, and power source of both short-axis strokes. It teaches you to use your hands to anchor (or hold on to your place in the water) far in front, then link your arms to the propulsive power available in your torso muscles.

Follow this sequence:

1. Start as in Drill #7.2 above. Every 2 to 4 pulses, slide your hands forward and apart to the "corners" (slightly wider than your shoulders).

2. Then slide the hands back together again. Don't allow the movement of your arms to interrupt the pulsing rhythm you've set up in your core body.

3. When the movement and timing feel natural, add a pause at the corners. Hold that pause until you feel your hips and legs skim the surface, then release the pressure on your chest and bring your hands together again. Take a breath as you bring the hands back together.

Experiment by changing the number of hand-lead pulses you take before sliding to the corners. Some swimmers feel more comfortable taking 2 or 3 pulses; others feel best when they slide to the corners on every other pulse. Some like to slide to the corners on every pulse. You can also vary the drill by taking a mini pull (quick scull) to bring your hands back together as you come up to breath.

Advance to the next drill when: You can easily anchor your hands at the corners every 2nd or 3rd pulse and feel a band of linked power from your fingers to your toes at the moment of greatest stretch. You can seamlessly fit this action into a full length of rhythmic body dolphins.

Lesson Eight: Butterfly Drills

Butterfly is the stroke most rarely swum well, yet when swum correctly it is the most beautiful of all strokes.

Butterfly can be so tiring that most anyone's stroke (except for elite swimmers) quickly degenerates into some form of "butterstruggle." But this lesson, modeled on what the best "flyers" do, can help anyone learn to swim at least a little bit — several strokes to a length or two — of fluent, relaxed butterfly through a series of drills that allow you to practice fluent movement with simple steps progressing gradually to whole-stroke butterfly. By following this progression, you can avoid swimming a single stroke of butterstruggle. *Always* begin with review of Lesson Seven.

Drill #8.1: Stoneskipper

Why do this drill: It teaches you to seamlessly add the butterfly armstroke and breathing to the core-body "wave" rhythm developed in Lesson Seven. Think of this drill as two Hand-Lead Body Dolphins followed by two Head-Lead Body Dolphins, with the "skip" as the link between the two. The "skip" acts in the same way as the "switch" in freestyle drills.

Follow this sequence shown on the next four pages.

1. First do at least one length of Hand-Lead Body Dolphin as in Drill #7.1 above. To turn it into Stoneskipper, pulse once with arms extended.

2. Then pulse once to the corners.

3. Anchor the hands, then take an underwater-only butterfly stroke, finishing the stroke at your hips (no recovery).

4. As you take the underwater butterfly stroke, keep pulsing and "skip" your chest over the water like a stone.

5. Pulse once with your arms at your sides, then release.

6. Pulse again and, as you release your chest, "sneak" your hands and arms back to the front.

7. Practice until you can fit the underwater butterfly "armstroke" and the breaststroke recovery into your body dolphins with no inturruption. Practice for short distances (two cycles) so that you don't have to breath. When your body dolphin feels fluid and rhythmic, fit the breath into it as follows:

- Breathe as *early* as possible in the stroke.
- Breathe with your head in a neutral position, looking down slightly. Your head should stay within the line of body movement.

- Land forward, not down, to finish the breath. Once you can fit the breath seamlessly into the stroke, breathe on every Stoneskipper cycle.

Drill #8.2: Hip-Delay Butterfly

Why do this drill: If you can avoid fighting gravity (lifting arms up and climbing out of the water), butterfly becomes much easier. This drill adds a flat, relaxed, sweeping recovery to the stroke and breathing skills learned above. Follow this sequence:

1. Start as in Drill #8.1 above. After the stroke, leave your arms at your sides and pulse twice more (Head-Lead Body Dolphins).

2. As you release from the second pulse, sweep the arms out to the sides and to the starting position. The sweep should be low, relaxed and non-splashy. It will take some experimenting to find the right moment in your pulsing rhythm to begin the recovery without feeling awkward. *When you get it right you should feel as if your arms just float over the water to the front.*

3. Continue breathing on every armstroke, but remain face down during the recovery.

Drill #8.3: Body-Dolphin Butterfly

Why do this drill: It integrates all the skills you worked on in the first two drills with armstroke, recovery, and breathing. The drill is simple: Keep your arms extended for two extra pulses before each stroke, but don't pause (as in hip-delay) When you take the stroke, concentrate on the following:

- **Stroke.** Pulse, stroke, and breathe just as in Stoneskipper, but instead of pushing the arms back, flare them out *early* and to the side to start the recovery. This should feel as if you are making a karate chop out to the sides with your hands.

- **Recovery.** Wide and flat. Feel as if you are sweeping the arms forward until you land head, arms, and torso together.

Land forward not down.

Let your forward momentum help you slide your hands effortlessly to the corners.

- **Breathing.** Breathe as early as possible in the stroke. Practice a *"sneaky breath,"* as if trying to hide your breath from an observer. Keep your head in line with your spine and look down during each breath.

- **Low Profile.** Keep your head and shoulders as close as possible to the water's surface. Imagine trying to fit the stroke and breath under a very low ceiling.
- **Pulsing.** Don't let taking a breath or moving your arms interrupt the pulsing rhythm you've set up in your core body. Fit everything into your core-body rhythm.

Drill #8.4: Swim Butterfly (EZ Fly)

Why do this drill: Put the whole stroke together — *no butterstruggle.*

Practice tips: Swim just three to six non-breathing full strokes at the start of each length — only as many strokes as you can take and still feel smooth and in control.

As soon as your stroke feels even slightly rough, switch to a short-axis drill (anything from Lesson 7 or 8) or swim any other stroke the rest of the way. This makes it much easier to execute all the skills learned in butterfly drills. Once your technique feels good, add one or two breaths. As you practice, focus on the following:

- "Sneaky breaths." Keep your head in line with your spine and look down slightly as you breathe.
- Keep your recovery wide, flat, low, and relaxed.
- Land forward, not down.
- Don't take a single stroke of "butterstruggle."

Practice Tips for Lesson Eight

1. Always begin fly drill practice with at least a few refresher lengths of Lesson Seven drills. They are so valuable to imprinting a relaxed rhythmic core-body undulation that they helped set a world record. In August 1999, just before breaking the 100-meter butterfly record (the oldest standing WR at the time), Jenny Thompson was doing Head-Lead Body Dolphin in the warmup pool just before climbing to the blocks for her race.

2. For novice flyers, Slim Fins can be a huge aid in gaining control and learning to do your drills with ease. To gradually wean yourself from fins, simply practice the drills for shorter distances or fewer cycles and build distances patiently.

3. As the drills become "no-brainers," you can build them into "drill progressions" by swimming one length of each drill – in the order in which they are presented in this book. Once you've reached the most advanced drill, return again to the most basic drill and start the learning sequence again. Always avoid *butterstruggle*.

4. If you are a novice butterflier and want to swim it in a meet, but are uncertain of your ability to swim the whole distance, both Drill #8.2 and #8.3 are legal forms of whole-stroke butterfly, either to swim the entire race distance or to use as a "rest" when your whole-stroke becomes too much like butterstruggle.

Lesson Nine: Breaststroke Drills

Before learning or practicing any of the following breaststroke drills, spend a few laps reviewing the drills in Lesson Seven. This will help establish short-axis balance and coordination before you move on to a more difficult skill. Refer to the video *BUTTERFLY AND BREASTSTROKE: The Total Immersion Way* for the best guide to these drills.

Drill #9.1: Heads-Up Pulling

Why do this drill: The fastest way to master a quick and efficient breaststroke pull – one that keeps you moving FORWARD – is to practice with your head above the water. This teaches you to keep your pull compact and your head steady, and to spin your hands quickly to the front. This drill is most effective when done with tremendous focus and intensity for very short distances.

Key Points:

• Look down slightly at all times. Feel as if you're wearing a neck brace. You stay low, you look down, but your goggles never touch the water.

• The pull is quick and compact. In order to maintain good rhythm, use a small dolphin kick. Drive your arms forcefully to the corners.

- Take a quick, powerful, and compact pull, and spin your hands directly to the front again.
- During the pull, keep your hands and arms in front of your shoulders.

- In fact, try to keep them as far forward as possible, even while spinning your hands quickly out and together again.

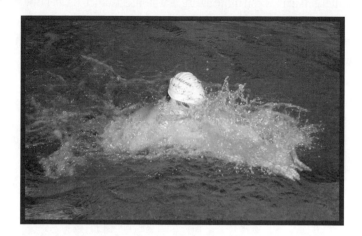

- Keep your elbows as high as possible on the outsweep. Hunch your shoulders forward on the insweep.
- See your hands fully extended before your chin is back in the water.
- Keep a constant core-body rhythm as you practice.

Drill #9.2: Underwater Kick

Why do this drill: This is the best way to develop a more effective kick. Being submerged makes you more aware of water resistance on all body surfaces.

Key Points:

- Start by pushing off deeper than usual and keep your arms streamlined forward the whole time you're underwater. Start with just two to three kicks on each drill cycle.

- Use your sense of the water's "thickness" to stay as slippery as possible. Keep your arms streamlined overhead and travel as far as you can after each kick. Slip your body through the smallest possible "hole" in the water as you glide.

- Most important, "sneak" your legs forward on recovery inside the same space your body traveled through.

- Also use that resistance to develop more thrust from your kick. Because the water feels more "solid" while kicking under water, experiment with positioning your legs and feet to create maximum thrust.
- Finish each kick by **squeezing** all the water out from between your legs and feet, then hold your streamline and feel some glide before sneaking your legs up again to start the next kick.

Drill # 9.3: One Up, Two Down

Why do this drill: To direct the energy in each stroke forward, increasing stroke length in each breast cycle. To emphasize slipping the body through the smallest possible hole in the water, just below the surface, during the glide phase.

Follow this sequence:

* Start each length with two underwater kicks, arms streamlined forward. Glide a bit after each kick (but not so long that you lose momentum).
* Resurface by taking a quick, compact pull (similar to Drill #9.1) with breath.
* Make the pull and breath quick and low, and keep moving forward. Imagine you are slipping under a low ceiling.
* After the pull and breath, slice back into the water with a super-streamlined, forward-darting movement (imagine *piercing* the water) to maximize forward momentum and minimize drag. The hands can be just at the surface of the water, or slightly beneath the surface.

- Imagine you are slipping your needle-like body through a narrow tube just above (as you pull and breathe) and below (during the two kicks) the surface.

- Keep the extra underwater kick in every cycle of breast. While under water, emphasize good thrust and a long glide on both kicks.

Drill # 9.4: One Up, One Down (Swim Breaststroke)

This isn't really a drill, just a way to swim breaststroke with heightened focus on efficiency and specifically to bring the awareness created in the previous three drills into your whole-stroke swimming. It is the natural finishing touch to the progression in these four steps.

Follow this sequence:

Simply start with Drill #9.3 and take out the extra kick. With what remains, focus on the following:

1. Make your glides extra-long and super-streamlined, "threading the needle" while under water.

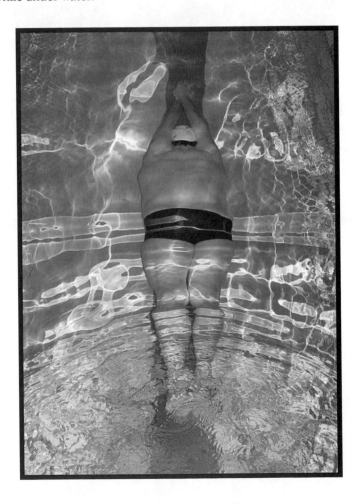

2. A quick, compact pull with the hands always in sight.

3. Breathe with your head aligned with your spine and looking slightly down. Imagine you're wearing a neck brace.
4. *Pierce* the water with hands, arms, head, and torso after each breath.

Drill # 9.5: Body-Dolphin Breaststroke

Why do this drill: It will emphasize core-body movement (undulation) in your breaststroke.

Follow this sequence:

1. First review Hand-Lead Body Dolphin for one or several lengths.
2. Start each breaststroke cycle with one hand-lead chest pulse, and using a dolphin kick.

3. Release the chest (but don't take a breath)...

4. ... then pulse again, driving your hands to the corners...

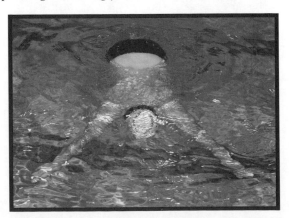

5. ... and directly into a cycle of regular breaststroke swimming with a breast-stroke kick.

6. Finish the cycle of breaststroke with hip action exactly the same as in the chest pulse at the beginning, *i.e.*, with a dolphin kick.
7. Glide for a moment before beginning the next cycle with another chest pulse.
8. The more emphatic and powerful the chest pulse at the beginning of the cycle, the stronger will be the body wave at the end. Your practice should focus on making the chest press/hip lift at the completion of each cycle feel more identical to that at the beginning, and a more natural part of your whole-stroke swimming.

Practice Tips for Lesson Nine

These five drills combine to form a natural and logical practice progression when done in sequence. They are also extremely effective when any of the drills are alternated with lengths of whole-stroke swimming. Whenever you swim, simply take the insight or awareness made most apparent by the drill and apply it to your whole-stroke swimming.

Lesson 10: Short-Axis Combinations

Our final lesson combines butterfly and breaststroke in ways that will give you unprecedented insights into how to use core-body undulation for breathing, power, and propulsion in both strokes. Doing alternating cycles of the two short-axis strokes, both drilling and swimming, creates a synergy that works like magic to improve each individual stroke and your overall awareness of how to relate to and work with the water. Indeed it does this to a greater extent than is possible when practicing only the drills of one stroke.

Again, it's easier to understand the subtle dynamics of these drills by combining the visual reinforcement of the video *BUTTERFLY AND BREASTSTROKE: The Total Immersion Way* with the instructions below.

Drill # 10.1 Body-Dolphin Combo

Why do this drill: It will help you better understand how to use core-body undulation to provide the power and rhythm for both butterfly and breaststroke.

Follow this sequence:

1. Begin with one or two hand-lead pulses, then slide to the corners and breathe with a fly stroke. As the hands enter the water, flow immediately into one or two hand-lead pulses, then slide to the corners and breathe with a breaststroke pull. Use dolphin kick on the butterfly cycle, and breaststroke kick on the breaststroke cycle.
2. As you practice, focus on making the timing and breathing the same in both strokes.
3. In both strokes, let the pulse drive your hands to the corners and into the stroke.

4. In both strokes, you keep your head as close as possible to its natural position at all times.
5. In both strokes, channel your momentum *forward*, not down, after the stroke.
6. You can practice this in long, leisurely, relaxed repeats, alternating a fly stroke and a breast pull, after each pair of body dolphins. The more you practice, the more strongly you imprint length, relaxation, and fluency into your strokes.

Drill # 10.2: Short-Axis Combo Swimming

Why do this drill: Our final drill is the most challenging of all, but once you master it, fishlike swimming in either butterfly or breaststroke will be natural and effortless.

Follow this sequence:

1. Start with two (or three) strokes of butterfly, then take two (or three) strokes of breast, then go back to fly again.
2. You can work on staying low and long if you don't breathe on fly. Get your air on the two cycles of breast. Then go back to fly again, just keeping your head in line with your spine.
3. On one length, start with butterfly. On the next start with breast.
4. Use the fly cycles to imprint more *hip action* in your breaststroke. Use the breast cycles to imprint more *stroke length* in your butterfly.
5. Try to keep a steady, unbroken, unhurried rhythm through both strokes.

This completes our lessons, but there are endless creative combinations you can do with the various drills to become steadily more Fishlike and fluent. Practicing the drills in combination with each other and with whole-stroke swimming will help imprint the lessons even more strongly.

Short-Axis Progressions

Here are some sample combinations and progressions that we really like. Practice a full 25 yards of each drill before switching to the next drill. Then go on to try other creative combinations of your own design.

*   Start with Hand-Lead Body Dolphin…then practice Body-Dolphin Breast…and finish with One Up, One Down.
*   In another sequence, start with Heads-Up Pulling…progress to One Up, Two Down…and finish with One Up, One Down.

- A third breast sequence starts with Underwater Kick, progresses to One Up, Two Down, and finishes with One Up, One Down.
- For a fly sequence, combine Head-Lead Body Dolphin… followed by Stoneskipper…and finish with EZ Fly.
- Another fly sequence combines Hand-Lead Body Dolphin…Body-Dolphin Butterfly…and EZ Fly.
- Our final progression begins with Body-Dolphin Combo…segues to SA Combo Swimming…switches to One Up, One Down…and finishes with EZ Fly.

Afterword
Time To Swim

The goal of this book has been simple: to start you on a lifetime process of learning to swim all four strokes better, to make you ever more efficient and economical in the water. And it *will* do that for you. But along the way, the Total Immersion program will accomplish more than simply making you a much-improved swimmer. Little by little, you'll also discover how to:

- Determine the ways in which you, as an individual, can best use your pool time to produce constant improvement, every minute, every practice.
- Experience unparalleled enjoyment with every stroke you take.
- Use the perpetual process of refining the art of swimming to bring your mind and your body into closer harmony—*out* of the pool as well as in it.

The building blocks of this process, as we've said over and over again, are the special Total Immersion drills. That is why most of the program in this book has concentrated on them as the tools of choice to refine your skills and heighten your body awareness. At some point, however, you obviously need to move up to practicing whole-stroke swimming, to polish the full skill as the sum of its parts. Whole-stroke practice develops the ability you need to blend the building blocks seamlessly under faster and faster circumstances, i.e., an improved time for your regular mile-swim routine or successful racing in competitive swimming or triathlon.

When you do begin practicing whole-stroke swimming, focus on just two things:

1.   How good your movements feel.
2.   How efficiently you are moving.

In a minute we'll review what a "good" movement should feel like in each stroke. But for now, just remember this: Your body has a highly developed ability to distinguish between desirable and undesirable movements; *efficient movement always feels better*. If someone tells you, for instance, that you can't possibly swim freestyle well with your head down "that low" in the water, that you have to hold your head high to ride high, *put it to the test.* Don't accept either prescription as gospel; try both. Swim a short distance with your head in line with your spine. Then swim a similar distance with your head held higher, and compare how each feels. Your body knows; learn to trust it. And don't be afraid to do things wrong now and again, even on purpose. It can only help to develop your "internal compass"— your instinctive gauge of what's right and what's not — into a more discriminating instrument.

To gauge your efficiency, get in the habit of counting strokes, whenever you are not focusing on one of the kinesthetic sensations described below. For stroke counting, remember that your goal is not to *maximize* your Stroke Length (i.e., reduce your strokes per length ever closer to zero), but to *optimize* it. In other words, your goal is to find the style of swimming that allows you to swim with a controlled and consistent stroke count with the least effort. As your practice teaches you to increase control and consistency and reduce effort, you'll be able to improve your SL, or increase your SR a bit without a major loss of SL (i.e., go faster without a serious increase in stroke count). Developing this ability to freely move your stroke count up and down while maintaining control and fluency is a key skill to getting ready for more serious and ambitious training.

How Your Strokes Should Feel

"That's nice," you say. "My body is constantly reporting in to me, as I swim, what I'm doing right and what I'm doing wrong. But how am I supposed to know what it's telling me?" Glad you asked. Here's how to sort out the important messages, and what you want to be hearing from that "internal compass" of yours:

Fishlike Freestyle

Start with a long, sleek, balanced bodyline. Slice through the water with a shape that is as close to needle-like as possible at all times, even while stroking. Use your hands to make your needle shape longer and to hold on to your place in the water. Move faster by rolling that long, slippery vessel back and forth faster.

How to Know if You've Got It Right
Body/Head Position
- Feel as if a thin film of water could wash over the back of your head at any time.
- Lead with the top of your head, not your nose. Watch the bottom directly *under* you and not *in front of* you.
- Swim "downhill" by leaning on your chest, shifting that pressure from side to side with your body roll.
- Slip a long, clean bodyline through the smallest possible "hole" in the water.
- Use rhythmic weight shifts to provide rhythm, tempo, and power.

Arms
- -Lengthen your body with "weightless arms."
- Slide your arm into the water as if into a sleeve, Continue extending until your shoulder touches your jaw, just below your ear.
- "Switch" your hands in front of your head with the same timing as in the "switch" drills.
- *Anchor* your hand and hold on to the water as if you were pulling your body past a rung on a ladder. (Use fistgloves ® frequently to heighten your ability to feel this sensation without the gloves on.)
- Avoid arm churning; let body rhythm drive your stroke. Try to make the speed of your hands match the speed of your body.

Legs
- Kick with a long, supple line; keep legs inside your body's wake or "shadow."
- Do not let your kick become too vigorous or overt – unless you are sprinting.

Fishlike Backstroke

A fishlike backstroke, just as in freestyle, is swum mainly on the side. But because power and leverage are limited when you're "upside down and going backwards," it's even more important to be slippery. To swim faster, roll your long, slippery vessel back and forth faster ("Move your bellybutton faster.") rather than churning your arms faster. Keep your body position stable by keeping your head completely still. You can reinforce this by occasionally drilling or swimming with a half-filled water bottle on your forehead.

How to Know if You've Got It Right

Body/Head Position

- To stay slippery and balanced, lean on your upper back as you rotate from side to side.
- If you are balanced, each rotation will bring a "dry patch of thigh" clear of the water.
- *Hide your head*, keeping it slightly tucked and fixed.
- Roll both shoulders clear of the water on every stroke cycle to maximize body roll.

Legs

- Kick with a long, supple leg, with no knee bend and with feet toed-in slightly.
- Remember that your kick rotates as your body rolls, and the beat is generally more steady than in freestyle.
- Keep your legs inside your body's "shadow."

Arms

- Keep the recovering arm straight but relaxed. ("Extend your fingertips toward the ceiling.")
- Emphasize a long bodyline as your hand slices cleanly and deeply into the water.
- Hold the water with your hand, then throw water toward your feet. (The fistglove® stroke trainers can be more valuable in backstroke than in any other stroke.)
- Keep arms exactly opposite each other and linked to body-roll rhythms.

Fishlike Butterfly

Think long, low, and relaxed. The secret of efficient, effortless butterfly is to stay close to the surface at all times; *don't fight gravity!* Keep your head, hands, and shoulders as close to the surface as possible on the stroke and recovery. Imagine you are swimming under a very low ceiling. Breathe *forward*, not up, keeping your head in a neutral position. Sweep the arms on recovery, and land *forward* after recovery. The deeper you dive on re-entry, the shorter will be your bodyline and the steeper your climb back out.

Next in importance is to keep your head aligned with your spine and to look down slightly throughout the stroke. Breathe without raising or jutting your chin; breathe inside the line of the stroke. Drill and swim with little or no overt kick. Your legs should be driven by body movement — chest pulses — not by thigh muscles. Bottom line: Swim butterfly with your body, not with your arms and legs.

How to Know if You've Got It Right

Body/Head Position

- Maintain a long, balanced, supple bodyline.
- Swim as close to the surface – both above and below – as possible; channel your energy *forward*, not up and down.
- Keep your head as close as possible to a neutral position at all times; use "sneaky breaths."

Legs

- Minimize overt kicking and leg bend; let the legs follow core-body undulation.

Arms

- Land *forward* on entry; don't hammer down or dive down after the recovery.
- Anchor hands at corners, then move your body over your hands.
- Sweep the hands in high on your chin, then immediately flare them out for a "karate-chop" exit.
- Recover the arms in a relaxed, sweeping motion.

Breathing

- Breathe early in the pull, without raising or jutting the chin.
- Look down slightly (take a "sneaky breath").

Fishlike Breaststroke

Stay *long and streamlined*. The single most important thing you can do to maximize stroke efficiency is to streamline your entire body as you finish each stroke. Use your arms to lengthen your body, whether for just a split second in a sprint, or slightly longer when swimming a longer distance. The second-most-critical key to efficient breaststroke is a neutral head position. Keep your head aligned with your spine during and after each breath; if you raise or jut your chin during the breath or thrust it down after the breath, you'll compromise your bodyline, stroke length, and power.

Always think *forward* as you swim breaststroke. Pull forward, breathe forward, land forward, and kick forward. Lead the forward thrust with your fingertips. Where they go, your body will follow. Except during the underwater pull, your hands never push water toward your feet. The breast pull is exclusively out-and-in sweeps leading to a strong forward-attacking drive.

How to Know if You've Got It Right

Body/Head Position

- Maintain a long, streamlined, balanced bodyline.
- Look down slightly as you breathe, and keep your head in line with your spine.
- Breathe with body lift (on the insweep), not by lifting your chin. (It helps to imagine you're wearing a neck brace.)
- Keep a constant short-axis body-rocking rhythm — slower when swimming slowly, and speeding up by undulating your chest and hips faster.

Legs

- "Sneak" the legs up inside the "hole" made by your core body, on recovery.
- Turn your heels in, toes out, and "grab" as much water as possible at the beginning of the kick, then push the water back with a somewhat ovoid motion.
- At the finish, point your toes, "clap" your feet, and squeeze all the water out from between your legs.

Arms

- Keep your pull compact and quick; better too small than too big.
- Always keep hands where you can see them. Keep them as far for-

ward as possible during every phase of the pull.

- Sweep your hands to the corners, then spin them directly back to meet in front.

Timing

- Reach full extension in every stroke.
- Help your recovery timing by *kicking your hands forward.*
- Try to have your hands reach full extension at the same moment your face is back in the water.
- Adjust your rhythm in the core, not in your arms and legs.

It may have surprised you to find this book makes next to no use of a word you'd normally expect to see all over a publication about improving your swimming. The word, of course, is "training." And its absence is intentional. In everything we've covered here, I've wanted to draw a clear distinction between the two parts of preparation to swim better. The first — and most critical — step is to learn to move with coordination, control, and fluency, and to polish those movements into instinctive habits. The second part — and the one that will ultimately have much less impact on how well you swim — is to build the fitness, endurance, and strength to be able to move like that for longer periods, at higher speeds.

So let me suggest in closing a new definition of swimming endurance. Because you can waste far more energy through inefficient movement than you could ever provide through workouts, think of swimming endurance as *"the ability to repeat highly efficient swimming movements for a duration of your choosing, at a range of speeds, stroke rates, and heart rates."* Notice that "strength" or "power" would be only part of that definition, and the smaller part at that, taking a distant back seat to technique.

Still, there's no question that training helps. And just as there are right ways and wrong ways to work on technique, there's good and not-so-good training. Before long, I plan to write a separate book that will offer comprehensive advice on how to train intelligently and in a very practical way. But in the meantime, it's the technique work in this book that will help you hit the improvement jackpot faster than any conditioning program ever could.

So for now, as I like to say to all my campers, I wish you "Happy Laps."

Index

Order Form for Total Immersion Products

Total Immersion offers weekend workshops year round and nationwide, as well as videos, books, website, and more than a dozen carefully chosen products that we believe will truly improve your swimming. To order any of our products or to enroll in a Total Immersion weekend workshop, call 800-609-7946 (845-256-9770 from outside the USA) or visit us online at www.totalimmersion.net. The following discount packages can be ordered by phone, online, or by mailing/faxing the order form on the next page. A shipping-and-handling charge of $5.90 will be added to each order shipped within the USA; charges will be higher for international orders.

Freestyle and Backstroke: The Total Immersion Way $49.95
PAL version is $54.95

This 40-minute instructional video provides clear images and complete instructions for the balance drills taught at a TI workshop, and that are described in *Swimming Made Easy*. Key points of each drill are illustrated in slow-motion, surface, and underwater views.

Butterfly and Breaststroke: The Total Immersion Way $49.95
PAL version is $54.95

This 45-minute instructional video provides clear images and complete instructions for the short-axis drills described in *Swimming Made Easy*. Key points are shown in slow-motion, surface, and underwater views.

Pool Primer for Freestyle and Backstroke: The TI Way $29.95
26 waterproof, spiral-bound pages • Convenient 5 1/2 X 8 1/2-inch format • full color throughout

The perfect companion to our *Freestyle and Backstroke* video and *Swimming Made Easy*. Use the video to get a visual image of how our unique drills should be performed. Use *Swimming Made Easy* for background and complete *written* instructions for our drills. Then take the waterproof *Pool Primer*, which distills and illustrates the key points of TI's special drills, to the pool to guide your practice.

Swimming Made Easy:
The *Total Immersion* Way for *Any* Swimmer to Achieve Fluency, Ease, and Speed in *Any* Stroke, by Terry Laughlin $24.95
224 pages paperback format

Package #1	**$89.95**	**Package #4**	**$50.00**

Package #1   **$89.95**
• Freestyle/Backstroke video
• Butterfly/Breaststroke video
                    (PAL price is $99.95)

Package #4   **$50.00**
• *Pool Primer for Freestyle and Backstroke*
• *Swimming Made Easy*

Package #2   **$75.00**
• Freestyle/Backstroke video
• *Pool Primer for Freestyle and Backstroke*
                    (PAL price is $80)

Package #5   **$125.00**
• Freestyle/Backstroke video
• Butterfly/Breaststroke video
• *Pool Primer for Freestyle and Backstroke*
• *Swimming Made Easy*
                    (PAL price is $135)

Package #3   **$100.00**
• Freestyle/Backstroke video
• Butterfly/Breaststroke video
• *Swimming Made Easy*
                    (PAL price is $110)

			Quantity	**Total**
Package #1	**$89.95**	(PAL version is $99.95)	_____	_____
Package #2	**$75.00**	(PAL version is $80.00)	_____	_____
Package #3	**$100.00**	(PAL version is $110.00)	_____	_____
Package #4	**$50.00**		_____	_____
Package #5	**$125.00**	(PAL version is $135.00)	_____	_____

NY State residents add 7 3/4% sales tax   _____

                                  US Shipping $5.90

                                                      TOTAL   _____

Name: _____

Address: _____

City/State/Zip: _____

Province/Country: _____

Phone: _____ Fax: _____

E-mail: _____

Credit Card: ☐ VISA ☐ MC ☐ AMEX ☐ DINERS ☐ DISCOVER

CC Number: _____

Expiration Date: _____

Signature: _____

Fax form to: 845-256-0658 • Or Mail to: Total Immersion
Make all checks payable to: **171 Main Street**
   Total Immersion, Inc.   **New Paltz, NY 12561**